Contents

Northern Ireland

London: H M S O

Researched and written by Reference Services, Central Office of Information.

This publication is an expanded and updated version of a booklet with the same title previously published by the Foreign & Commonwealth Office.

HMSO publications are available from:

HMSO Publications Centre
(Mail, fax and telephone orders only)
PO Box 276, London SW8 5DT
Telephone orders 071-873 9090
General enquiries 071-873 0011
(queuing system in operation for both numbers)
Fax orders 071-873 8200

HMSO Bookshops
49 High Holborn, London WC1V 6HB   071-873 0011
Fax 071-873 8200 (counter service only)
258 Broad Street, Birmingham B1 2HE   021-643 3740   Fax 021-643 6510
Southey House, 33 Wine Street, Bristol BS1 2BQ
0272 264306   Fax 0272 294515
9-21 Princess Street, Manchester M60 8AS   061-834 7201   Fax 061-833 0634
16 Arthur Street, Belfast BT1 4GD   0232 238451   Fax 0232 235401
71 Lothian Road, Edinburgh EH3 9AZ   031-228 4181   Fax 031-229 2734

HMSO's Accredited Agents
(see Yellow Pages)

and through good booksellers

Photo Credits
Numbers refer to the pages in the illustration section (1–4): Derek Cattani p. 2 (bottom), p. 3 (top), p. 4 (bottom); David Page p. 3 (bottom).

[Front cover] The Giant's Causeway. David Page.

Introduction

Northern Ireland is part of the United Kingdom. With a population of some 1.5 million, it consists of six of the nine counties of the old Irish Province of Ulster.

The majority of people in Northern Ireland are descendants of Scots and English settlers who crossed to the north-east of Ireland, mainly in the seventeenth century. Most are Protestants, British by culture and tradition and committed to maintaining the constitutional link with the British Crown. The remainder—just over a third—are Roman Catholic, Irish by culture and history and favour union with the Irish Republic.

Northern Ireland had its own Parliament between 1921 and 1972. The Unionists—primarily representing the Protestant community—held a permanent majority in this Parliament and hence formed the regional government which had full responsibility for local affairs with the exception of defence and the armed forces, foreign and trade policies and taxation and customs.

Because of increasing street violence and terrorism in the late 1960s and early 1970s, the British Government at Westminster assumed direct responsibility for Northern Ireland affairs and security in 1972.

Since then, successive British Governments have sought—so far without success—to establish the framework for a locally accountable Northern Ireland administration commanding widespread support throughout the Protestant and Roman Catholic communities. The Government recognises the need to involve the minority community in any such arrangements and, at the same time, upholds the principle that there should not be any change in Northern Ireland's constitutional status as part of Britain without the consent of a majority of the population in the Province. The Northern Ireland Constitution Act 1973, for instance, states that ' . . . in no event will Northern Ireland or any part of it cease to be part of . . . the United Kingdom without the consent of the people of Northern Ireland voting in a poll'. This principle of consent is also affirmed by the 1985 Anglo-Irish Agreement (see p. 67).

History

In the twelfth century Henry II invaded Ireland and part of the country came under the control of Anglo-Norman barons. By the end of the thirteenth century, there was an Irish Parliament but with increasingly scant allegiance to the King of England. In 1541 Henry VIII took the title 'King of Ireland', and during the reign of Elizabeth I a series of campaigns was undertaken to subjugate Catholic Ireland to safeguard English security interests. Schemes were drawn up to settle the land and substantial numbers of Scots and English arrived in the northern province of Ulster. This was the main area of resistance and once this was overcome early in the seventeenth century, an attempt was made to consolidate control over Ireland.

During the English civil war and after (1642–52) further risings in Ireland were crushed by Cromwell, who extended the colonisation by English and Scots settlers. The Catholic James II came to the throne in 1685 but was defeated at the Battle of the Boyne in 1690 by the Protestant William of Orange. In 1782 the Irish Parliament was given legislative independence but Ireland continued to be constitutionally linked with England, Scotland and Wales under the Crown. The Parliament represented, however, only the upper classes, mainly of settler origin, who owned most of the agricultural land, and the native Roman Catholic majority was excluded from it. Following the abortive United Irishmen rebellion, in which disgruntled Ulster Presbyterians played a major part, Ireland became part of the United Kingdom under the 1800 Act of Union. The Irish Parliament was abolished in 1801, the whole of Ireland being governed from London with Irish representation in both Houses of the British Parliament.

During the nineteenth century the nationalist demand for Irish independence continued and by the end of the century there was a well-organised movement for Irish home rule which sought devolved government by constitutional means. With Irish nationalists holding the balance of power in the House of Commons, a Home Rule Bill was introduced by Liberal Prime Minister Gladstone in 1886 but failed to get parliamentary approval because of opposition by some members of his party. A second bill was introduced in 1893 but this was rejected by the House of Lords.

Pressure for home rule continued but there was resistance by the Unionists, who in 1912 organised the signature of a covenant against home rule. This was followed by the formation of a Unionist militia called the Ulster Volunteer Force. Irish Nationalists also formed a militia, the Irish Volunteers.

After the 1910 general elections the Asquith Government was dependent on support from the Irish Parliamentary Party which pressed for another home rule bill. Home rule was, thereupon, enacted in 1914, but, with the outbreak of the first world war and the threat of armed resistance by the Ulster Unionists, its implementation was suspended. The Government stated that, before applying the legislation, Parliament would have an opportunity to make special provision for Ulster by amending it.

In the south of Ireland various forces were demanding a stronger measure of separation than that contained in the Home

Rule Bill. The 1916 Easter Rising in Dublin, which proclaimed the Irish Republic, was a turning point; although it attracted little support at first, revulsion at the execution of some of its leaders by the British Government stiffened Republican opposition.

In the 1918 general election the Republican Sinn Fein ('Ourselves alone') swept the board in Ireland outside Ulster by winning 73 of the 105 Irish seats and crushing the Parliamentary Nationalist Party. The elected Sinn Fein members boycotted the Westminster Parliament by forming the first Dail Eireann (Parliament) in Dublin, which reaffirmed the 1916 proclamation of the Republic made by the Easter rebels.

This direct challenge to the authority of the British Crown led to hostilities between Sinn Fein's military wing—the Irish Republican Army (IRA)—and the Royal Irish Constabulary, supported by auxiliary forces.

The British Government decided to concede the demand for Home Rule, but to a limited extent since it was still strongly opposed by Ulster Protestants who wanted to maintain the Union and remain part of the United Kingdom. The 1920 Government of Ireland Act provided for separate Northern and Southern Irish Parliaments within the United Kingdom. Although the Act was implemented in Northern Ireland in 1921, it was ignored in the South where hostilities continued until July 1921 when a truce was declared. Negotiations between the British Government and Sinn Fein led to the signature of the Anglo-Irish Treaty in December 1921.

Following the Treaty in 1922, the Irish Free State was established as a self-governing dominion with the same constitutional status as Canada, Australia and New Zealand. Under the Treaty members of the Dail were obliged to swear an oath of allegiance to the British monarch, and the Irish Free State Government gave facilities for use by British warships. A minority in the Dail, led by Eamon de Valera, opposed the 1921 Treaty. A bitter civil war then followed in 1922 and 1923 between the Free State forces and the anti-Treaty forces of the IRA which were forced to surrender.

In 1937 the Irish Government under the leadership of Mr de Valera introduced a new constitution which asserted the Irish claim to the six counties of Northern Ireland and changed the Irish Free State's name to Eire. The remaining formal links with the United Kingdom were gradually dissolved and in 1949 Eire left the Commonwealth and became the sovereign Irish Republic.

Recent Northern Ireland History

After 1921 a majority of the voters in Northern Ireland voted in successive elections for a Unionist Government pledged to maintain the province's constitutional position as part of the United Kingdom. Unionists felt confirmed in this view both by the Irish Republic's claim that the national territory consisted of the whole of Ireland, and by IRA terrorist campaigns during the second world war and between 1956 and 1962.

On the other hand, Roman Catholics, who felt excluded from the administration of the state and distanced from Northern Ireland as a political entity, remained mainly nationalist and continued to favour a united Ireland outside the United Kingdom. Consequently, the Unionist/Nationalist issue tended to dominate Northern Ireland politics, often to the exclusion and to the detriment of social and economic problems.

Continuing allegations of discrimination by Unionist-dominated local councils in the allocation of jobs and housing and in the formation of local government electoral boundaries led to the emergence in 1967 of an active broad-based civil rights movement. The aim of the movement was to win social and electoral reforms so as to place Roman Catholics on an equal footing with Protestants. A series of marches and rallies was organised by the campaigners in 1968. Simultaneously, so-called Loyalist extremists sought to resist these campaigns by violent protest, as they saw reforms as weakening the previous Unionist ascendancy.

By August 1969 serious sectarian disturbances led the Northern Ireland Government to request London to provide additional support for the severely over-stretched police force. Although at first welcomed by the Roman Catholic community, the presence of Army reinforcements was exploited for propaganda purposes by the IRA which mounted a series of attacks. In the early 1970s, after the Provisional IRA had broken with the Official IRA, the nature of the violence changed fundamentally from a public order problem to a terrorist one.

Reform Programme
In response to the civil disorder which followed the human rights campaign, a reform programme was implemented. This included:

—the reorganisation of the police and the establishment of a representative police authority;

—the introduction of universal adult suffrage for local council elections and the reorganisation of local government;

—the setting up of a new housing authority and the introduction of a points system for the allocation of public housing; and

—measures to prohibit employment discrimination by public bodies.

Terrorist Organisations

The most severe threat to law and order comes from the Provisional IRA, whose ultimate aim is to force British withdrawal from Northern Ireland. It hopes that, as a result of its violence and the consequent political stagnation, some future British Government, under pressure from the British electorate, will conclude that the social, economic and political costs of remaining in Northern Ireland are such that the constitutional link cannot be sustained. To that end the Provisional IRA has over the last 20 years or so conducted a campaign of murder, bombing and violence, financed by a mixture of legal and illegal activities, the latter including armed robbery, extortion, fraud and other racketeering. Funds are also received from overseas sources, including the Irish Northern Aid Committee—NORAID—in the United States. There is also clear evidence that Libya has in the past supplied arms and explosives to the Provisionals.

Another republican terrorist organisation is the Irish National Liberation Army which, although much smaller than the Provisionals, has been responsible for some particularly ruthless acts of terrorist violence and murder.

In retaliation against republican terrorism, so-called 'loyalist' paramilitary groups were formed in the early 1970s from within the Protestant community. The Ulster Defence Association was formed from various vigilante groups set up in 1971. The terrorist Ulster Volunteer Force and the Ulster Freedom Fighters have bombed and murdered Roman Catholics. Waves of 'tit for tat' killings have taken place. The 'loyalist' terror groups finance their activities by racketeering along similar lines to that of the Provisional IRA.

Republican and 'loyalist' terrorist organisations are banned by law; membership is a criminal offence punishable by imprisonment.

Terrorist acts, from whatever source, have been condemned by political leaders, by church representatives of all faiths and by the great majority of the community.

About 3,000 people, mostly innocent civilians, have died since 1969 as a result of terrorist campaigns. Bombs have been exploded in crowded places such as public houses and shops. Many deaths have resulted from sectarian shootings in the victims' homes in front of close relatives. Hundreds of people have been injured by so-called punishment shootings designed to terrorise individuals and communities. The level of violence, however, is lower than in the early 1970s—in 1991, for instance, there were just under 100 deaths compared with 467 in 1972. The security services continue to have major successes against the terrorists and it is thought that they manage to prevent about 80 per cent of planned terrorist attacks.

From 1973 the Provisional IRA extended its terrorism to Great Britain, where some 100 people have been murdered, including three Members of Parliament. In 1984 a bomb exploded in a Brighton hotel where members of the Government were staying during the Conservative Party Conference; the explosion killed five people. In 1991 a mortar attack was aimed at the Prime Minister's official residence in Downing Street, where a Cabinet meeting was taking place. The Provisional IRA also extended its campaign to British military installations and interests in mainland Europe where a number of British servicemen were killed.

Efforts to Obtain a Political Settlement

Because of the violence and terrorism, the British Government decided in 1972 to assume direct responsibility for law and order. The Northern Ireland Government refused to accept this decision and resigned. A Secretary of State was appointed to administer Northern Ireland. The regional Parliament at Stormont, near Belfast, was abolished in 1973.

Since the introduction of direct rule, successive British Governments have taken a series of initiatives in the search for political progress. Without prejudice to the differing aspirations of the two political traditions in Northern Ireland, both Conservative and Labour Governments have tried to establish a locally elected administration acceptable to both parts of the community.

In 1973 a new 78-member Assembly was elected by proportional representation and in 1974 a broadly based Executive was set up, its members drawn from the Assembly. The Executive was composed of Unionists and members of the Nationalist Social and Democratic Labour Party (SDLP) and representatives of the cross-community Alliance Party. In December 1973 the British and Irish Governments and the Northern Ireland Executive-designate agreed to establish a Council of Ireland to give institutional recognition to 'the Irish dimension'. In the communiqué issued after the meeting, which was held at Sunningdale, the Irish Government declared that there could be no change in the status of Northern Ireland until a majority of people in Northern Ireland desired a change in that status. The British Government confirmed that it would remain its policy to support the wishes of the people of Northern Ireland.

The Executive took office on 1 January 1974 and worked well for a time. The new arrangements, especially the Council of

Ireland, were resented by many Unionists. Unionists opposed to the Executive won 11 of the then 12 Northern Ireland House of Commons seats in the February 1974 general election. In May a mass 'loyalist' protest strike against the Executive took place, this leading to the resignation of the Chief Executive, Mr Brian Faulkner. The Executive was prorogued and direct rule returned.

In May 1975 a constitutional convention was elected to consider 'what provision for the Government of Northern Ireland is likely to command the most widespread acceptance throughout the community there'. Fundamental differences, however, emerged between Unionists and the SDLP and the Convention was dissolved in March 1976 following the failure of both sides to agree a compromise.

In 1982 the Government introduced a new initiative designed to restore devolved government. The Northern Ireland Act 1982 provided for the resumption of legislative and executive functions by an elected Northern Ireland Assembly if agreement could be reached on how these powers should be exercised. The proposed arrangements, the Government emphasised, would have to command widespread acceptance throughout the community and be acceptable to the United Kingdom Parliament. In the meantime the Assembly was given monitoring, scrutinising and consultative functions intended to make direct rule more accountable to local needs and allow elected representatives to contribute to the day-to-day government of Northern Ireland. It commented upon a large quantity of draft legislation and initiated reports on education and industry.

The 78-member Assembly was elected in October 1982 under the single transferable vote system of proportional representation. From the start neither the SDLP nor the Sinn Fein members took their seats. After the signature of the Anglo-Irish Agreement in November 1985, the Unionist representatives suspended the Assembly's monitoring work as part of their protest against the Agreement. In December 1985 the Alliance Party withdrew from the Assembly in protest against the Unionist decision. In March 1986 the Assembly decided formally not to fulfil its statutory functions and in June 1986, after the refusal of the two main Unionist parties to discuss the situation, the Government dissolved the Assembly.

The Government remains committed to the principle of a locally accountable administration acceptable to, and enjoying the support of, both sections of the community. In 1989–91 the Secretary of State had a series of discussions with constitutional politicians representing Unionists and Nationalists. The talks were set up to discuss the relations within Northern Ireland, between the peoples of the island of Ireland and between the British and Irish governments. Formal political talks were held during a ten-week period between 30 April and 3 July 1991. Initially, bilateral exchanges took place between the constitutional parties on procedural issues which were eventually resolved. Plenary sessions started on 17 June. Position papers were presented by the parties for discussion. The talks were brought to a conclusion by the Government with the agreement of the participants because they could not be completed by the end of the ten-week period.

Further talks between the parties have resumed. To facilitate this exercise, the British and Irish governments agreed in April 1992 to a three-month break in meetings of the Anglo-Irish Intergovernmental Conference.

Relations with the Irish Republic

Successive British governments have believed that links with the Irish Republic are beneficial to Northern Ireland—for example, co-operation on security, transport and economic development. Particular importance is attached to security co-operation between the authorities on both sides of the border and for many years there has been co-operation in energy, transport, communications, tourism, agriculture, fisheries and other economic developments. A variety of institutions are organised on an all-Ireland basis, for instance, various sporting bodies, the Irish Congress of Trade Unions, the Roman Catholic Church and the Presbyterian Church of Ireland. There is also a common travel area between Britain and the Irish Republic and close family, cultural, educational, commercial and sporting ties. In addition, there are reciprocal voting rights. Both countries are members of the European Community which gives financial aid for the joint development of certain border areas.

In 1981 an Anglo-Irish Intergovernmental Council was set up to meet regularly at ministerial and official levels to discuss matters of common concern.

The Anglo-Irish Agreement

On 15 November 1985 the British and Irish Governments signed the Anglo-Irish Agreement (see p. 67) which is binding in international law.

It affirms that any change in Northern Ireland's status can only come about with the consent of a majority of its people. It recognises that at the present time a majority does not want any change in status. The Agreement also states that, if, in the future, a majority clearly wishes for and formally consents to a united Ireland, both governments would promote legislation to that effect.

The Agreement established an Intergovernmental Conference in which the Irish Government is able to put forward views and proposals on Northern Ireland questions, as long as these are not the responsibility of a devolved government. The Conference meets regularly in full session. It has discussed:

—cross border security co-operation between the two police forces against terrorism;

—the elimination of discrimination, particularly in employment;

—relations between the security forces and the community in Northern Ireland;

—legal, social and economic matters;

—human rights; and

—the use of the Irish language.

The Agreement commits both governments to seek to resolve differences between them. Each, however, retains responsibility for decision taking in its own jurisdiction. A secretariat services the Conference.

Although the Agreement was generally welcomed by the minority Nationalist community, opposition among Unionists was widespread on the grounds that it has given the Irish Republic undue influence in the internal affairs of Northern Ireland and that it is a step towards a united Ireland against their wishes. The British Government considers that the Agreement offers benefits to both communities without detracting from the rights of either. Both Governments have made it clear that they would be prepared to consider a new and more broadly based agreement or structure if such an agreement can be arrived at through direct discussion and negotiation between all the parties concerned, including the constitutional parties in Northern Ireland.

Administration

The Northern Ireland Office is the United Kingdom Government Department in which the Secretary of State, assisted by four other Ministers, has overall responsibility for Northern Ireland. The Secretary of State is directly responsible for political and constitutional matters, security policy, broad economic questions and other major policy issues. Responsibility is shared among the other ministers for the Departments of Agriculture, Economic Development, Education, Environment, Finance and Personnel, and Health and Social Services. The functions of the various departments are as follows:

—*Department of Agriculture*: development of agricultural, forestry and fishing industries; rural areas; veterinary scientific and advisory services; administration of European Community and other support arrangements; agricultural education and training.

—*Department of Economic Development*: development of industry and commerce, as well as administration of government policy in relation to tourism, energy, minerals, industrial relations, employment equality, consumer protection, health and safety at work and company legislation; administration of an employment service and labour training schemes through the Training and Employment Agency; and assistance to industry through the Industrial Development Board.

—*Department of Education*: control of the five education and library boards and education as a whole; youth services; sport and recreation; cultural activities and community services and facilities, including the improvement of community relations.

—*Department of the Environment*: housing; planning; construction and maintenance of roads; transport and traffic management and motor taxation; water and sewerage; environmental protection; ordnance survey; collection of rates; harbours; historic monuments and buildings; maintenance of public records; and certain controls over local government.

—*Department of Finance and Personnel*: control of public expenditure; liaison with the Treasury in London and the Northern Ireland Office on financial matters, economic and social planning and research; charities; valuation and lands service; policies for equal opportunities and personnel management; and general management and control of the Northern Ireland Civil Service.

—*Department of Health and Social Services*: health and personal social services; social security; social legislation; and the Office of the Registrar-General.

Local Government

There are 26 elected district councils responsible for local services including street cleaning, refuse disposal, consumer protection, environmental health and the provision of recreational facilities. Councils nominate locally elected representatives to sit as members of the various statutory bodies which administer regional services such as education and libraries, health and personal social services, drainage, fire services and electricity.

All candidates at district council elections are required to sign a declaration to the effect that, if elected, they will not support terrorism or assist proscribed organisations.

Citizens of the Irish Republic who are able to vote in Northern Ireland parliamentary elections are also able to do so in local government elections.

Parliamentary Elections

Northern Ireland elects 17 of the 651 members of the House of Commons at Westminster. At the most recent general election in April 1992 the 17 seats were distributed between the parties as follows: Ulster Unionist 9, Democratic Unionist 3, Ulster Popular Unionist 1 and Social and Democratic Labour 4. The Alliance party, set up to offer an alternative to Unionist and Nationalist parties, failed to win a seat. Sinn Fein lost its single seat to the Social Democratic and Labour Party.

The leader of the Ulster Unionists is the Rt Hon James Molyneaux, MP and the Democratic Unionist leader is the Revd. Ian Paisley MP. Mr John Hume MP is leader of the SDLP. Dr John Alderdice is leader of the Alliance Party.

Three of the 81 United Kingdom representatives in the European Parliament are elected in Northern Ireland on the basis of proportional representation. At the elections held in 1979, 1984 and 1989 the Democratic Unionist, the Social Democratic and Labour and the Ulster Unionist parties each won one seat.

Human Rights

The British Government is unequivocally committed to the protection and enhancement of human rights in Northern Ireland, where people enjoy the same basic rights as other people in the United Kingdom. Since 1969 a number of measures have been introduced to protect human rights and to prevent discrimination in the public and private sectors on the grounds of religious belief. Areas covered include local electoral law, local government, law and order, housing, fair employment and the appointment of an Ombudsman.

The independent Standing Advisory Commission on Human Rights examines the adequacy and effectiveness of the law regarding religious and political discrimination in Northern Ireland and makes recommendations to the Government. The Commission reports annually to Parliament.

Fair Employment

In 1976 a law was passed which outlawed direct discrimination in employment on grounds of religious belief or political opinion. It established a Fair Employment Agency with powers to investigate, and adjudicate upon, complaints of discrimination and to conduct investigations into the extent of equality of opportunity in Northern Ireland.

Figures published by the Government in mid 1985 showed that a wide differential continued to exist in the employment opportunities of Protestants and Catholics. The Government therefore strengthened the law through the Fair Employment (Northern Ireland) Act 1989 which came into operation in January 1990. The Agency was renamed the Fair Employment Commission and given additional resources to meet its new commitments. The Act also made indirect discrimination illegal.

Under the Act all private sector employers with more than 10 employees must register with the Commission; all public authority employers—irrespective of size—are treated as registered. These private and public employers must submit annual returns to it on the religious composition of their workforces. They must also review their recruitment, training and promotion practices at least once every three years. Failure to comply with these obligations is a criminal offence; if an employer is summarily convicted, a fine of up to £2,000 can be imposed. Economic sanctions, for example, loss of government grants and contracts, are also available.

The Act also empowers the Commission to direct an employer to take affirmative action and set goals and timetables where fair participation by both communities in employment is not being secured. Affirmative action measures may include encouraging job applications from an under-represented group. The Commission has power to:

—disqualify defaulting employers, thereby bringing them within the scope of economic sanctions;

—seek High Court injunctions to stop the placing of contracts with a disqualified employer;

—audit employers' monitoring and review functions; and

—support individuals alleging discrimination.

The Commission also maintains a Code of Practice which sets out detailed recommendations for employers, trade unions and others. It also gives advice, on request, to employers on their review of practices.

The main powers of the new Fair Employment Tribunal set up by the 1989 Act are to:

—decide individual cases of alleged discrimination;

—award compensation of up to £30,000 to compensate individual victims of discrimination; and

—recommend remedial action by employers to correct discrimination.

The Tribunal is also concerned with fair employment practices. It has powers to:

—hear appeals from employers against directions of the Commission;

—issue enforcement orders and impose cash penalties of up to £30,000; and

—certify the employer to the High Court for failure to obey its orders. The High Court has unlimited powers of fine and committal.

The Act is evaluated continuously and will be reviewed formally after five years.

Table 1: Composition of Northern Ireland Workforce by Standard Occupational Classification and Sex

	Male workforce						Female workforce						Total workforce					
	Public sector		Private sector		Total male		Public sector		Private sector		Total female		Public sector		Private sector		Total workforce	
	P %	RC %	P %	RC %	P %	RC %	P %	RC %	P %	RC %	P %	RC %	P %	RC %	P %	RC %	P %	RC %
SOC1 Managers and administrators	71·4	28·6	71·6	28·4	71·8	28·5	66·1	33·9	62·0	38·0	64·0	36·0	69·7	30·3	69·4	30·6	69·5	30·5
SOC2 Professional occupations	71·1	28·9	69·3	30·7	70·3	29·7	59·5	110·5	56·5	43·5	58·6	41·4	66·9	33·1	66·0	34·0	66·6	33·4
SOC3 Associate professional and technical occupations	61·3	38·7	75·0	25·0	67·2	32·8	53·5	46·5	60·9	39·1	54·7	45·3	56·1	43·9	70·0	30·0	59·9	40·1
SOC4 Clerical and secretarial occupations	55·5	44·5	73·0	27·0	65·1	34·9	61·5	38·5	71·1	28·9	66·1	33·9	60·2	39·8	71·7	28·3	65·9	34·1
SOC5 Craft and skilled manual occupations	70·6	29·4	67·0	33·0	67·7	32·3	68·3	31·7	57·0	43·1	57·0	43·0	70·5	29·5	64·8	35·2	65·7	30·3
SOC6 Personal and protective service occupations	83·5	16·5	63·1	37·0	80·0	20·0	60·1	39·7	58·1	41·9	59·5	40·5	74·6	25·4	60·3	39·7	71·5	28·5
SOC7 Sales occupations	75·9	24·1	68·7	31·3	68·9	31·1	73·5	26·5	65·0	35·0	65·2	34·8	74·2	25·8	66·5	33·5	66·7	33·3
SOC8 Plant and machine operatives	63·5	36·5	63·5	36·5	63·5	36·5	76·4	23·6	57·5	42·5	57·6	42·4	63·8	36·2	61·1	38·9	61·4	38·6
SOC9 Other occupations	58·5	41·5	60·4	39·6	59·4	40·6	61·7	38·3	65·1	35·0	63·2	36·8	60·1	39·9	62·3	37·7	61·2	38·8
Overall %	69·6	30·4	67·0	33·0	68·0	32·0	59·6	110·4	63·0	37·0	61·5	38·5	64·7	35·3	65·3	34·7	65·1	34·9
Total numbers	50,582	22,083	77,620	35,896	123,202	57,979	41,567	28,217	49,922	29,070	91,489	57,287	92,149	50,300	122,542	64,966	214,691	115,226

NB. Percentages shown in this table relate only to those individuals for whom a community was determined.

Source: *Fair Employment Commission 1990 Monitoring Returns.*

In 1990 the Commission received returns from 101 public sector employers employing 154,845 people and from 1,758 private sector employers covering 194,555 employees. Overall the composition of these employees was 214,691 (61·4 per cent) Protestant, 115,266 (33 per cent) Roman Catholic and 19,443 (5·6 per cent) Non-Determined. The composition of those for whom a community was determined was 65·1 per cent Protestant and 34·9 per cent Roman Catholic. Table 1, taken from the Fair Employment Commission's annual report for 1990–91, gives the composition of the work force by standard occupational classification and sex.

The Commission's returns for the public sector (see Table 2, p. 24) showed that Roman Catholics occupied 35 per cent of senior positions in the education and library boards, 29·5 per cent in the Housing Executive, 22 per cent in the health and social services boards, 21·2 per cent in the district councils and 18·6 per cent in the Northern Ireland Civil Service.

Sex Discrimination

It is unlawful to discriminate on grounds of sex or against married people in employment or on grounds of sex in the provision of goods, facilities and services. The Equal Opportunities Commission for Northern Ireland helps to enforce the sex equality legislation and promotes equality of opportunity between the sexes generally. It encourages employers to adopt positive action policies for women and to implement equal opportunities programmes.

Table 2: Composition of Public Sector Senior Staff

	Protestant		Roman Catholic		Other		Total
NICS	2,028	(69·3%)	543	(18·6%)	355	(12·1%)	2,926
		[78·9%]		[21·1%]			
Northern Ireland Electricity	1,113	(81·9%)	228	(16·8%)	18	(1·3%)	1,359
		[83·0%]		[17·0%]			
Health and Social Services Boards	752	(59·4%)	278	(22·0%)	236	(18·6%)	1,266
		[73·0%]		[27·0%]			
District Councils	503	(75·1%)	142	(21·2%)	25	(3·7%)	670
		[78·0%]		[22·0%]			
Northern Ireland Housing Executive	390	(64·4%)	179	(29·5%)	37	(6·1%)	606
		[68·5%]		[31·5%]			
Education and Library Boards	293	(53·2%)	195	(35·4%)	63	(11·4%)	551
		[60·0%]		[40·0%]			
OMCS	208	(58·4%)	70	(19·7%)	78	(21·9%)	356
		[74·8%]		[25·2%]			
Others	5,287	(68·4%)	1,635	(21·1%)	812	(10·5%)	7,734
		[76·4%]		[23·6%]			
Total	6,283	(68·2%)	2,021	(22·0%)	903	(9·8%)	9,207
		[75·7%]		[24·3%]			

Note: The figures in square brackets express the percentage of the total of Protestants and Roman Catholics only.

Source: *Fair Employment Commission Annual Report, 1990–91.*

Public Order

It is a criminal offence to incite hatred against a section of the community on the grounds of religious belief, colour, race or ethnic or national origin.

Complaints Systems

The Northern Ireland Parliamentary Commissioner for Administration deals with complaints by the public against maladministration by central government. The Commissioner for Complaints deals with complaints against other public bodies and local government authorities. Both offices are held by the same person. Powers of investigation are comprehensive and any person who obstructs the Commissioner can be dealt with by the High Court.

Complaints to the Parliamentary Commissioner are made through a Member of Parliament at Westminster. Complaints can be made direct to the Commissioner for Complaints.

Proportional Representation

Other measures to safeguard human rights have included the introduction of proportional representation for local government elections and for Northern Ireland elections to the European Parliament.

Community Relations

Northern Ireland is a deeply divided society, the origins of which are rooted in several hundred years of Irish and British history. The conflict between Protestant and Catholic in Northern Ireland continues to divide the community and much of the violence and political instability flows from this. The Government's community relations policy endeavours to bring the two sides closer towards greater understanding.

The main objectives of the policy are to:

—ensure that everyone enjoys equality of opportunity and equity of treatment;

—increase the level of cross-community contact; and

—encourage greater mutual understanding of, and respect for, the different cultures and traditions.

Community Relations Programmes

Government spending on community relations has increased from £1·2 million in 1988–89 to over £7 million in 1992–93. Support is given to the Community Relations Council, an independent body set up to promote community relations work in Northern Ireland. The Council's budget is just over £1·5 million in 1992–93 and it can make grants to other bodies. It has 21 members representing a broad spectrum of community interests, of whom one third are appointed by the Government.

In 1992–93 the Government is providing the district councils with £1·3 million for locally based programmes which encourage cross-community contact, mutual understanding and awareness of cultural diversity and which command cross-party support. Twenty-two out of a total of 26 councils are participating. Another £800,000 is being set aside to support the work of a number of reconciliation bodies which promote cross-community contact and the creation of more tolerant and harmonious communities.

In addition, the European Community has agreed to provide some £9 million for community reconciliation projects. One of the main objectives of this EC programme is to reduce community tensions within the region in order to bring about a resolution of tension and conflict.

Community Relations and Education

Two cross-curricular themes—Education for Mutual Under-standing and Cultural Heritage—are compulsory elements of the school curriculum, applying to all 300,000 children in full-time education between the ages of 5 and 16.

Under the Schools Cross Community Contact Scheme, over 500 schools and around 350 youth and community groups have come together voluntarily to pursue joint work. About a third of all schools are working together, in pairs or larger clusters, on projects covering common curricular areas of study (see p. 53). The scheme has been recently extended to include parents.

Some £1·9 million is spent annually on a Cultural Traditions Programme, which is aimed at encouraging greater understanding of different cultural traditions in Northern Ireland and showing that differences do not have to lead to division. A major element of the programme is encouraging people from each of the main traditions to encounter and appreciate the culture of the other.

Research

A wide ranging research programme aims to maintain an up-to-date body of information on the nature and effects of the major divisions in Northern Ireland and to evaluate, assess and report on the impact of Government policies, including those on community relations.

Law and Order

The Police

The Police Authority for Northern Ireland, an independent body whose members are appointed by the Secretary of State, has a statutory duty to maintain an adequate and efficient police service. There is one police force—the Royal Ulster Constabulary (RUC)—which is controlled and directed by its Chief Constable.

From its inception in June 1922, the RUC has had a dual role—providing a service of law enforcement similar to that of other police forces in the rest of Britain while at the same time protecting the state from armed subversion. This necessitates the carrying of firearms by police officers for their self-protection. Nearly 300 police officers have been murdered by terrorists and thousands injured.

The regular RUC has over 8,200 officers. The RUC Reserve assists the police on a full-time or part-time basis. It has some 4,500 members, of whom 3,000 are full-time.

The RUC's ten ranks are similar to those of other British police forces. The regular force is open to all law abiding British citizens and to natives of the Irish Republic. All regular recruits have 14 weeks initial training, following which they complete a two-year probationary period before their appointments are confirmed.

Police officers must operate within the law and are liable to prosecution in the same way as any other members of the community if they break it. Any complaint alleging criminal misconduct by a police officer is investigated by the Royal Ulster Constabulary. The RUC Chief Constable must submit every police criminal investigation report to the Director of Public Prosecutions (DPP) who decides whether criminal proceedings should be brought.

The Independent Commission for Police Complaints for Northern Ireland receives copies of all complaints made by members of the public against police officers. The Commission is required to supervise the police investigation of the more serious complaints and, at its discretion, may supervise the investigation of any other complaints against a police officer. At the end of any supervised investigation, the Commission must state whether or not it is satisfied with the way the investigation was carried out. In addition, if the Commission disagrees with a decision of the Chief Constable not to take disciplinary action in respect of any complaints, it may direct that such action be taken.

In 1990 the RUC's rate of crime detection was 37·5 per cent which exceeds the average in England and Wales. Offences recorded by the RUC per 100,000 population fell by 12 per cent between 1981 and 1989. An international survey carried out in 1988 showed that overall levels of crime in Northern Ireland were the lowest in Western Europe and below those in the United States, Canada and Australia.

The Armed Forces

The Army supports the RUC in the fight against terrorism. Ten Regular Army units (normally infantry battalions) are deployed in Northern Ireland. In addition, there are seven Ulster Defence Regiment (UDR) battalions with 3,000 permanent personnel and

3,000 part-time soldiers. At the beginning of July 1992, the UDR merged with the Royal Irish Rangers to form a new regiment of seven Home Service battalions and one general service battalion. The part-time element is being retained.

Members of the armed forces, like the police, must operate within the law. In the case of complaints against the Army where the RUC considers a criminal offence has been committed, it submits a report to the DPP who decides whether or not to prosecute; in the absence of criminal proceedings the Army authorities may take disciplinary action.

In 1991 the Army established an office to improve the monitoring and handling of complaints against the armed forces. Under the Northern Ireland (Emergency Powers) Act 1991, the Office of Independent Assessor of Military Complaints Procedures is being created to scrutinise and review complaints procedures against military personnel made by the public.

Emergency Legislation

In order to protect the public and maintain order, Parliament has passed legislation intended to give the security forces and civil authorities additional powers to deal with and prevent terrorist activity. The main legislation is composed of two Acts. The Northern Ireland (Emergency Provisions) Act 1991 (EPA), apart from a few minor exceptions, applies only in Northern Ireland, and the Prevention of Terrorism (Temporary Provisions) Act 1989 (PTA) has effect throughout the whole of Britain. Each Act is subject to annual review by an independent rapporteur. The temporary provisions of each Act must be renewed annually by Order of Parliament.

The EPA, which has a maximum life of five years, provides the legal basis for the continuation of the so-called 'Diplock' Courts, in which terrorists prosecuted for certain offences scheduled in the Act are tried by a single High Court judge sitting without a jury. These courts were introduced in 1973 on the advice of the report of an independent commission chaired by Lord Diplock. Before 1973 jurors had been intimidated and, on occasion, murdered. The Attorney General retains the discretion, however, to send certain cases for trial by jury and has increasingly done so in recent years.

Apart from the absence of a jury in cases involving scheduled offences, the legal process is similar to that in ordinary criminal courts. Trials are held in open court, the prosecution must prove guilt beyond reasonable doubt, and the accused has the right to be represented by a lawyer and to cross-examine witnesses. In the event of conviction, the judge must set out his reasons in writing, a requirement that is unique in the British legal system. This can be of considerable assistance to the defendant if he or she is considering an appeal. The defendant has an automatic right of appeal against conviction on any ground and/or against sentence. Appeals are always heard by three judges. These procedures conform to the principles of the European Convention on Human Rights and the United Nations Covenant on Civil and Political Rights. Acquittal rates in the Diplock Courts are about the same as in the jury courts, that is, just under 50 per cent.

In 1988 the general criminal law in Northern Ireland regarding evidence was amended. A court is now allowed, in certain circumstances, to take account of the fact that the accused has remained silent when questioned before or during a trial and to draw whatever inferences appear appropriate from that fact.

Legislation passed in 1975 gives courts in Northern Ireland the power to try people accused of committing terrorist acts in the Irish Republic; reciprocal legislation is in force in the Republic.

Under the EPA and the PTA the security forces have powers to question, arrest and detain people suspected of being involved in terrorism. They also have powers of search and seizure of property, including vehicles. Certain terrorist organisations are proscribed under each Act; this has the effect of making it a criminal offence to be a member of, or to demonstrate support for, such an organisation.

Those suspected of terrorist offences may be detained for questioning for up to seven days. A suspect may only be detained longer than 48 hours with the written authority of the Secretary of State for Northern Ireland. Before the seven days expire, the person detained must either be charged or brought before a court on remand or be released. The general rule that the police must charge when they have sufficient evidence to do so continues to apply. In practice, most suspects are either charged or released well within the seven day limit.

Under the EPA a suspect has a general right of access to a solicitor and to have a person informed of their arrest and whereabouts. The exercise of these rights may only be denied under certain strict conditions. Following charge, bail will be granted unless the prosecution can present substantial grounds for believing that the person would, if released, fail to surrender to custody, commit an offence, interfere with a witness or obstruct the court.

The 1991 EPA introduced a new offence of directing, at any level, the activities of an organisation which is concerned in the commission of acts of terrorism. The offence carries a maximum penalty on conviction of life imprisonment. Under the Act it is also a crime to take part in racketeering organised by or for the benefit of terrorists; proceeds arising from such crime can be confiscated by the courts.

The PTA gives the Secretary of State the additional power of issuing an exclusion order. The effect of such an order is to restrain the right of entry of particular persons either to Great Britain, Northern Ireland or the whole of the United Kingdom. Such orders are issued for a fixed period of three years. The person subject to the order has the right to request a review of that order and may make representations in writing to the Secretary of State.

Prisons

The aim of the Northern Ireland Prison Service is to 'hold in secure and humane confinement persons who have been given into custody by the courts and to reduce the risk of re-offending by encouraging them to take full advantage of the opportunities offered during their confinement'.

The average prison population in 1990 was 1,785. The average male sentenced prison population has shown a sustained decline from 2,269 in 1978 to 1,409 in 1990. The corresponding figures for females were 30 and 14 respectively. Some 50 per cent of prisoners currently serving sentences were convicted of criminal offences connected with terrorism. There are four prison establishments and a young offenders centre; four of these have been built since 1970.

All prisoners have been convicted for criminal offences. No-one is imprisoned for his or her political opinions or religious beliefs. Many have been convicted of murder and other offences of violence against the person. All prisoners are treated on the basis of their offence, sentence, behaviour and security risk.

The Government is committed to running a humane and flexible regime throughout the prison system in Northern Ireland. Inmates have daily exercise and association with other prisoners and regular opportunities for physical recreation, leisure activities, education and training. All prisoners may wear their own clothes. Convicted prisoners may have weekly visits in open conditions with family and friends while those on remand or awaiting trial may have up to three such visits a week. All prisons have a visitors' centre with facilities for refreshments and children's play areas. There are also pre-release, compassionate and summer and Christmas home leave schemes for eligible inmates in order to help maintain family links: in 1990–91, 1,635 applications for pre-release home leave were approved—about 90 per cent of applications received. In 1990 some 414 prisoners were allowed to spend Christmas with their families.

Relaxations in the criteria under which books, periodicals, musical tapes and records were censored before entering the prison have been introduced. Unless material is regarded as a risk to prison security, anything available to the general public is allowed in.

Prisoners have the right to expect the full range of health care available to any other individual in the community. Health care is provided by a team of full-time Medical Officers employed by the Department of Health, assisted by a number of general medical practitioners. The Prison Medical Service has regular access to consultant advice and to all the medical, surgical and psychiatric services available through the National Health Service.

A unit to deal with problem prisoners suffering from mental illness has been recently opened at Maghaberry Prison.

Prisoners serving fixed term sentences receive remission of 50 per cent of their sentence subject to good behaviour in prison. The level of remission for those convicted of terrorist-type offences on or after 16 January 1989 has been reduced to a third. In addition, a person who is serving a sentence of more than one year for such an offence and who is released on remission will serve the remainder of the sentence if sent to prison for committing another terrorist-type offence before the expiry of the first sentence. The start of the new sentence will then follow. This provision is designed to deter people released from prison from becoming involved in terrorism and, if reconvicted, to keep them out of circulation longer.

As in the rest of Britain, life imprisonment is the mandatory sentence for murder, the death penalty having been abolished for this offence. As a result of the murders committed by republican and 'loyalist' terrorists, prisons in Northern Ireland have to accommodate a high proportion of inmates sentenced to life imprisonment—24 per cent of the sentenced population at the end of March 1991. Such prisoners may, however, be released into the community on licence. This can, if necessary, be revoked and the individual required to return to prison. All life sentence cases are reviewed regularly by a Life Sentence Review Board after ten years of imprisonment and on occasions earlier. If the Board is satisfied that a prisoner fulfils criteria for release, a recommendation is made to Government ministers and the views of the judiciary are sought. The Board may recommend release or a further review in between one and five years' time. The Secretary of State takes the final decision to release a prisoner under licence.

After a provisional release date is set and before the Secretary of State will sign the licence, prisoners must successfully complete a nine month pre-release programme. Since 1984 some 220 life-sentence prisoners have been released in this way.

The Economy

Public Finance

Northern Ireland has parity, both of taxation and services, with England, Scotland and Wales in its financial relations. Because of a relative lack of resources, public expenditure in Northern Ireland, as in other economically deprived regions of the United Kingdom, is partly financed by transfers from the more prosperous regions. In order to maintain public services at levels similar to those elsewhere in the United Kingdom, an annual financial subvention is made each year by Parliament; this was £2,549 million in 1991–92. In recognition of Northern Ireland's special needs, the level of public expenditure per head is higher than in the United Kingdom as a whole. Total public expenditure on central government services was some £5,023 million in 1991–92.

Northern Ireland is one of the poorer regions of the European Community with 80 per cent of the average gross domestic product per capita in the Community in 1988. In 1989 gross domestic product per head was some 75 per cent of the United Kingdom average.

Structure of the Economy

Northern Ireland has a small regional economy. In terms of population size, it is the smallest of the United Kingdom standard regions. In 1989 the population was about 1·6 million, accounting for 2·8 per cent of the United Kingdom total. Around half the population is settled on the eastern seaboard, the centre of which is Belfast. The remainder of the region is predominantly rural in character. In 1990 it had a gross domestic product of around £10,000 million and a working population of approximately 700,000—equivalent to 2·1 per cent and 2·5 per cent respectively of the United Kingdom totals.

The economic fortunes of the Northern Ireland economy are closely linked with those of the national economy. Almost half its manufacturing output is sold to England, Wales and Scotland with about a further quarter sold locally. Trends in output, employment and unemployment tend to reflect overall United Kingdom trends. Northern Ireland's unemployment rate is, however, persistently higher than the rest of Britain. In January 1992, for instance, seasonally adjusted unemployment was 14·3 per cent of the workforce compared with 9·0 per cent in Great Britain.

Over the last decade employment in agriculture, construction and, in particular, manufacturing has declined. The decline in manufacturing was concentrated largely in the early part of the 1980s—a fall of 26·5 per cent, followed by a modest decline in 1983–86 with stability between 1986 and 1990. There has been a switch in emphasis towards services, although agriculture accounts for a higher proportion of jobs than in Britain as a whole. Employment in services increased by 9·4 per cent between 1985 and 1990; this was largely caused by growth in retailing, hotels and catering and business services.

Twenty-five per cent of manufacturing jobs are in the textile and clothing industries, compared with less than 10 per cent in Great Britain. The public sector accounted for 39 per cent of employment in June 1991 compared with 25 per cent in Great Britain.

According to the latest data available (September 1991) 71 per cent of employees were engaged in services, 19·5 per cent in manufacturing, 4·4 per cent in construction and 5·1 per cent in agriculture, forestry, fishing, energy and water supply.

Economic Development

An economic strategy document, *Competing in the 1990s: the Key to Growth* was published by the Department of Economic Development in April 1990. It was drawn up against the background of increasingly competitive world markets and the creation of the European Community's single market. The aim of the strategy is to achieve higher levels of growth, leading to stable long-term jobs. The primary focus of policy is to achieve international competitiveness.

As the strategy is implemented, the Government will endeavour to get the best value for the resources designed to improve business confidence—for example, help with marketing, exporting, design, quality, innovation and skills; it also assists companies with growth potential to make the best of their opportunities. The other main features of the strategy include:

—identifying and removing obstacles to growth;

—an intensified drive for inward investment;

—building up management and workforce skills;

—giving a new impetus to support for innovation, research and development; and

—targeting programmes, where necessary, on areas of social and economic deprivation and on the needs of the long-term unemployed.

Industrial Development

Two public bodies are responsible for industrial development. The Industrial Development Board (IDB) deals with companies with more than 50 employees and with inward investment. Firms employing fewer than 50 people are assisted by the Local Enterprise Development Unit (LEDU).

IDB seeks to encourage the introduction and development of internationally competitive companies in manufacturing and tradeable services in order to create conditions for growth in durable employment. The IDB can help companies with marketing, exporting, improved productivity and quality practices. Its full range of help is available to those companies with the greatest development potential and with the greatest prospect of long-term competitive growth. Where appropriate, this assistance may include capital grants, revenue grants, loans and share capital investment.

Cash grants are available to cover up to 30 per cent of the eligible costs of new buildings, machinery and equipment. Up to a further 20 per cent may be available to internationally mobile projects, if they locate in a high unemployment area.

The IDB also pays revenue grant, including assistance:

—related to the number of newly created jobs in internationally mobile projects;

—towards rental costs of factories (up to 100 per cent of rental costs for up to five years); and

—towards interest costs on loans from non-Government sources—available for 3 years at a broadly commercial rate followed by four years at 3 per cent.

The IDB can make venture capital, loan guarantees and equity participation available to suit the needs of a particular project.

Management incentive grants offer companies help with attracting and recruiting quality management.

The IDB offers grants towards the consultancy costs incurred by companies in analysing their competitive position and preparing a strategic plan.

The IDB's Marketing Development Grant Scheme offers companies financial assistance towards a range of marketing activities targeted at export markets. It aims to encourage a strategic approach to marketing and is available on a single component basis or as a package. Assistance is provided to companies of up to 200 employees at the grant rate of 40 per cent of eligible costs; those with 201 to 500 employees can be grant aided at the rate of 30 per cent of eligible costs. The maximum yearly sum paid to any company on a single-component basis is £30,000; for a package it is £60,000. Through the Northern Ireland Technology Centre, part of Queen's University, Belfast, the IDB provides a consultancy support scheme to help companies improve quality and design efficiency.

A major part of IDB effort is aimed at foreign investment. Well known United States companies operating in Northern Ireland include Ford Motor Company, Du Pont and Fruit of the Loom. Companies from the Far East include Daewoo of Korea, and Ryobi and Canon of Japan. Germany has been one of the main sources of European investment with six firms currently operating, including Hueco and Hoechst. French companies include Michelin, Montupet and Pernot Ricard.

LEDU aims to encourage enterprise and stimulate improvements in the competitiveness of new and existing small businesses within defined markets. Assistance is primarily aimed at areas such as training, marketing, quality, design and research and development. Information and advisory services are available to potential entrepreneurs in the pre-start-up phase and businesses in the start-up, low-growth and growth phases.

In the pre-start-up phase, development grants for product, process or market research, patents and so forth are available to a maximum of £1,000 at a rate of 50 per cent. Assistance of up to £3,000 may be available for those becoming self-employed for the first time, and assistance of up to £2,000 per job created may be available for those becoming first-time employers. Businesses with export potential may be eligible for up to £4,000 per job created. LEDU assistance is normally limited to a maximum of 30 per cent of overall project costs.

LEDU's Local Enterprise Programme aids the establishment of local enterprise agencies throughout Northern Ireland. These provide workspace for small businesses and a range of advisory and common services. Under the Property Developers' Scheme a shortfall grant may be available to the private sector for the provision of industrial workspace.

Training and Employment Agency

The Training and Employment Agency is responsible for vocational training and employment activities in Northern Ireland. It is an executive agency within the Department of Economic Development, with 1,700 staff and a budget of £172 million. The Agency aims to help improve companies' competitiveness and provide individuals with marketable skills to enable both to compete with their counterparts in the European Community and further afield.

The Agency provides schemes designed to improve and develop management skills for existing managers and for graduates seeking to follow managerial careers. The Consultancy and Advisory Service promotes the benefits of industrial training and offers advice to individual companies and business sectors. Under another programme, financial support is offered to companies seeking to introduce comprehensive training programmes.

The 12 training centres provide high-quality off-the-job industrial skills training for young people and adults. They also provide sponsored training for industry where a company identifies a particular training need or problem.

The Agency has several training measures to enable individuals to acquire nationally recognised vocational qualifications and to compete for jobs in the European Community and worldwide.

The Job Training Programme is employer-based and aims to address the needs of the long-term unemployed by offering opportunities for them to update existing skills or to acquire skills in a new field. In 1991–92 the Agency is aiming to provide over 5,000 places. The Youth Training Programme lasts for two years and is aimed at all 16- and 17-year-olds. It seeks to lay the foundation for a skilled, flexible workforce and to assist participants to make the transition from school to adult life. It is delivered by community workshops, employers, further education colleges and the Agency's training centres. In 1991–92 some 10,000 places are being provided.

Under the Action for Community Employment scheme, jobs are provided for the long-term unemployed and offer one year's work in areas such as environmental improvement, help to old and disadvantaged people and energy conservation. Nearly 10,000 places are being provided in 1991–92 through community organisations.

The Employment Service provides a comprehensive placement service for adult unemployed people, young people, disabled people and employers. In 1990–91 it placed nearly 43,000 people in jobs and provided training opportunities for just over 23,000 people.

Urban Renewal

Considerable public expenditure is being devoted to urban renewal in Belfast and Londonderry.

The Department of Environment is responsible for stimulating development and re-development in Belfast. It is responsible for the renewal of large rundown areas in the city centre and for environmental improvements. The Department operates the Urban Development Grant Scheme which encourages private sector projects; this scheme has generated £231 million of private investment at a private/public ratio of 3:1. In addition it manages the Belfast Enterprise Zone which offers special incentives to attract new jobs and investment; over 3,000 jobs have been provided and £42 million of private investment achieved. It also manages the Belfast Action Team Initiatives.

Nine action teams have been established in Belfast to tackle the problems of designated areas of multiple deprivation. The aim is to encourage community organisations to become directly involved in tackling the problems with support from the public sector.

The Laganside programme, run by the Laganside Corporation on behalf of the Department of the Environment, is a £450 million mix of government and private development along the banks of the River Lagan in the heart of the city.

Another scheme, called 'Making Belfast Work', is designed to alleviate the economic, educational, social and environmental problems in the most disadvantaged areas of the city through targeted programmes. In addition to Government departments' mainstream programmes in these areas, a further £123·6 million is being allocated from public funds for the six year period from 1988 to 1994. The strategy is designed to:

—increase job opportunities and develop new businesses;

—improve the ability of people to compete for jobs through training and education programmes;

—improve the environment and living conditions; and

—involve the community and the private sector in partnerships with Government.

In December 1988 the Government announced an urban programme for Londonderry. Known as the Londonderry Initiative, it has three main elements:

—a town-centre development programme aimed at triggering private sector investment in new shopping, offices and other urban facilities;

—a community action programme designed to create more job opportunities and to improve the employability of people in the most disadvantaged areas; and

—a promotional strategy for the city in partnership with Derry City Council. A Festival of International Events is being held in 1992.

Other developments in Londonderry include restoration work within the walled city, an expansion of harbour facilities on the River Foyle, upgrading of the regional airport at Eglinton, the recently completed £8 million expansion of Magee College and the construction of government offices at Dorman's Wharf.

Transport

A number of important infrastructure schemes designed to improve transport links are being undertaken with the assistance of about £100 million from the European Community's Regional Development Fund. These include:

—the relocation and modernisation of the Port of Londonderry;

—modernisation of Belfast Port's handling equipment, storage sheds and warehousing;

—the provision of a new cargo terminal at Belfast International Airport, as well as an extension to its east passenger terminal; and

—the provision of a new international arrivals and departure facility at Belfast City Airport.

On 27 April 1992 the British and Irish Governments announced that the Belfast to Dublin railway would be upgraded in a £66·5 million project. This will permit speeds of 90 miles per hour which will shorten journeys by 15 to 20 minutes. New signalling equipment and rolling stock will also be provided. The European Community has indicated that it will provide grant support of up to 75 per cent of the project's cost. The work will take about five years to complete. Both Governments regard the project as an important contribution to the expansion of North-South trade within the island of Ireland.

Agriculture

Agriculture, together with forestry and fishing, accounts for 4 per cent of the province's gross domestic product. In addition, the food processing and agricultural supply industries have an output value of around £1,300 million.

About two-thirds of agricultural output is exported, the rest of Britain remaining the predominant market. There are also important specialised markets for livestock products within the European Community and in the Middle and Far East.

Approximately 80 per cent of the Province's area is agricultural with a further 5·5 per cent afforested. Grassland covers 72 per cent of the 1·1 million hectares of agricultural land and mountain or rough grazing a further 18 per cent. Barley accounts for about 56 per cent of the 67,500 hectares of crops. Livestock production based on grass is therefore the mainstay of farming. There are around 1·5 million cattle and 2·5 million sheep. Livestock and livestock products accounted for almost 90 per cent of gross output estimated at over £850 million in 1991. Grazing livestock account for about 70 per cent of output and intensive livestock for about 18 per cent.

The largest 11 per cent of farms produce over 46 per cent of output. There are about 29,000 farms, of which 16,000 are very small, generally part-time farms contributing 13 per cent of the industry's output and occupying almost 30 per cent of agricultural land. The majority of the remaining 13,000 farms provide full-time work for one or at most two persons; of these farms, 5,800 are involved mainly in dairying, 5,100 in beef cattle or sheep and the remainder in crops, intensive livestock or in more mixed types of farming.

Labour productivity has increased by about 6 per cent a year in the past ten years or so.

The Department of Agriculture is responsible for administering agricultural education through its three colleges and the Faculty of Agriculture and Food Science at Queen's University, Belfast.

Tourism

A major review published in 1989 identified the potential for further development of tourism in Northern Ireland. As a result of the review a more market-led strategy is well underway and there are some encouraging signs that Northern Ireland is once again considered as a serious holiday destination.

In 1991, visitor numbers were 1,180,000, exceeding 1 million for the third successive year, despite difficult worldwide travel conditions. The 1991 figure was 2·8 per cent up on the previous year. The number of pure holiday visitors continues to rise; 1991 saw an increase of 18 per cent on 1990 levels to just over 260,000.

The Government has overall responsibility for tourism policy. The Northern Ireland Tourist Board is responsible for marketing Northern Ireland's tourism potential. It administers schemes designed to help develop quality infrastructure for tourists and is also responsible for tourism programmes sponsored by the European Community and the International Fund for Ireland.

International Fund for Ireland

The International Fund for Ireland was established by the British and Irish Governments in 1986 to promote economic and social advance and encourage contact and dialogue between nationalists and unionists throughout Ireland. It is administered by an independent board jointly appointed by the two Governments and is financed by international contributions. Donors include the United States, the European Community, Canada and New Zealand.

When determining priorities for spending programmes, the board takes account of the wishes of donors. The Fund gives priority to projects in the most disadvantaged areas in Northern Ireland and in the Republic's six border counties. It is committed to spending about 75 per cent of its resources in Northern Ireland.

Programmes financed by the Fund cover business enterprise, tourism, urban development, agriculture and rural development, science and technology, community relations and community-led economic regeneration initiatives. Support was offered to almost 2,300 projects in the year up to 30 September 1991.

Social Affairs

Education

The education system is administered centrally by the Department of Education and locally by five education and library boards which provide nursery, primary and secondary schools, schools for pupils with special educational needs and colleges of further education. The Department of Education finances the boards' expenditure. Education is compulsory for pupils aged between 4 and 16 years.

Schools

The main categories of school supported by public funds are as follows:

—*controlled schools*, provided by the education and library boards and managed through boards of governors. Running costs are met in full from public funds;

—*maintained schools*, which are mainly under Roman Catholic management and maintained largely by public funds. The schools are managed by boards of governors with overall general management from the Council for Catholic Maintained Schools (see p. 52);

—*voluntary grammar schools*, which may be under Roman Catholic or non-denominational boards of governors and are financed through the local management of schools formula funding arrangements by the Department of Education (see p. 53); and

—grant-maintained *integrated schools*, taking Protestant and Roman Catholic pupils and funded by the Department of Education.

All grant-aided schools include elected parents and teachers on their boards of governors.

Although all schools must be open to pupils of all religions, most Roman Catholic pupils attend Catholic maintained schools or Catholic voluntary grammar schools and most Protestant children are enrolled at controlled schools or non-denominational voluntary grammar schools.

There are a few independent fee paying schools.

The Council for Catholic Maintained Schools has responsibility for all maintained schools under Roman Catholic management which are under the auspices of the diocesan authorities and of religious orders. The Council's main objective is to promote high standards of education in the schools for which it is responsible. The membership of the Council consists of trustee representatives appointed by the Northern bishops, of people appointed by the Department of Education in consultation with the bishops, and of parents and teachers.

Integrated Education
The Government has a statutory duty, set out in 1989 legislation, to encourage integrated education as a way of breaking down sectarian barriers. There are 16 integrated schools with a total of 2,800 pupils.

An oil tanker under construction at Harland and Wolff, Belfast.

Advanced carpet printing technology at CV Carpets, Donaghadee.

Ambulancemen monitor a portable defibrillator, manufactured near Belfast. It analyses the heart to detect the presence of life-threatening rhythms.

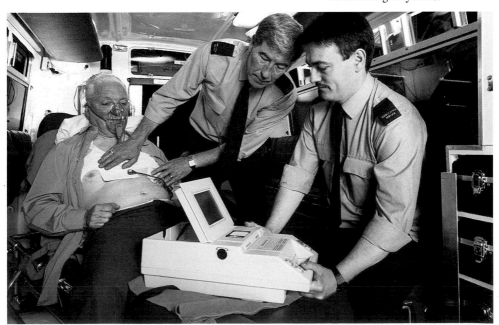

A high-tech building at the Antrim Technology Park.

Queen's University, Belfast.

A new Housing Executive development in Londonderry.

The Carrickfergus marina, opened in 1985.

New integrated schools receive immediate government funding. Existing controlled and voluntary schools can also apply to become integrated following a majority vote of parents. There are two categories of integrated schools:

—*grant-maintained integrated schools*, directly financed by the Department of Education and run by boards of governors; and

—*controlled integrated schools*, funded and supervised by the education and library boards.

Local Management

Local management of schools was introduced in 1991. Under this system, budgets for controlled and maintained nursery, primary and secondary schools are determined by formulae contained in schemes drawn up by the education and library boards. Secondary schools have full delegation and are responsible for deciding how they spend the whole of their formula-funded budget shares. Primary and nursery schools have only part delegation covering non-staff costs; staff costs are managed by the education and library boards. From April 1992, full delegation is being extended gradually into primary schools.

School Curriculum

A common curriculum is being introduced for all pupils aged 4 to 16 in grant-aided schools. Schools will be required to provide a curriculum made up of religious education and six areas of study—English, mathematics, science and technology, environment and society, creative and expressive studies and languages. Each area of study is made up of a number of subjects, some of which are compulsory. In addition, the curriculum for all pupils must also include a number of cross-curricular themes—Education for Mutual Understanding, Cultural Heritage, Health Education, Information Technology and, in secondary schools, Economic Awareness and Careers Education.

Schools will learn from a common history curriculum in the environment and society area of study. This will help pupils gain a better understanding of the other person's point of view by developing a greater knowledge and understanding of both the common roots and rich diversity of their historical heritage. The Department of Education provides modest grants to support schools pursuing programmes of joint work through its Cross-Community Contact Scheme (see p. 27).

Although schools are obliged to offer religious education and collective worship, parents have the right to withdraw their children from both. In controlled schools clergy have a right of access which may be used for denominational instruction. In voluntary schools collective worship and religious education are controlled by the management authorities.

The Northern Ireland Curriculum Council keeps under review all aspects of the curriculum.

There is formal assessment of pupils' progress at the ages of 8, 11, 14 and 16 (key stages 1 to 4), based on advice given by the Northern Ireland Schools Examinations and Assessment Council. Assessment results for key stages 1 to 3 are being obtained by a combination of continuous monitoring and external assessment. Assessment at key stage 4 will be through public examinations.

All pupils will be issued with a record of achievement on leaving primary and secondary education.

School Examinations

The main examination for secondary school children is the General Certificate of Secondary Education (GCSE) which is taken at the age of 16 after five years secondary education. This examination can lead to more advanced education and training. The General Certificate of Education (GCE) Advanced level is taken after a further two years' study. The Advanced Supplementary level examination enables sixth-form pupils to study a wider range of subjects than before. Advanced and Advanced Supplementary examinations are the main standards for entrance to higher education and to many forms of professional training.

The Certificate of Pre-Vocational Education is for those at school or college wishing to engage in full-time education for a year after the age of 16 and to receive a broadly based preparation for work or vocational and other courses.

Post-school Education

In 1989–90 just over 52 per cent of school leavers went on to some form of further or higher education; almost one third of these enrolled as first-year university undergraduates.

Queen's University, Belfast, provides undergraduate and post graduate courses in Arts, Economics and Social Sciences, Science, Law, Medicine (including Dentistry), Engineering, Theology, Education, Agriculture and Food Science.

The University of Ulster was formed in 1984 by the merger of the New University of Ulster, founded in the 1960s, and the Ulster Polytechnic. It has seven faculties—Art and Design, Business and Management, Education, Humanities, Informatics, Social and Health Services and Science and Technology. The

University offers graduate and postgraduate degrees as well as courses leading to various diplomas and professional qualifications. In addition, it has a significant number of non-degree courses designed to suit the needs of industry, commerce and the professions. It has four campuses at Coleraine, Jordanstown, Belfast and Londonderry and maintains close links with industry and commerce through its industrial unit which offers consultancy work.

Both universities have established an international reputation in engineering, information technology and bio-engineering. Local companies benefit from their consultancy services.

The Northern Ireland universities are an integral part of the United Kingdom higher education system. They are funded directly by the Department of Education on the advice of the Universities' Funding Council (UFC), the funding body for universities in the rest of Britain. The Council's advice is sought in order to ensure that provision in Northern Ireland is on the basis of parity with similar institutions in the rest of Britain. From April 1993 the UFC will be replaced by three higher education funding councils for England, Scotland and Wales. The Higher Education Funding Council for England will provide advice to the Department of Education on funding for the Northern Ireland universities.

The Open University operates throughout the United Kingdom, offering part-time degree and other courses through a combination of correspondence courses, television and radio broadcasts, summer schools and local study centres. The University has a regional office in Northern Ireland. The Department of Education contributes to all the University's costs incurred in Northern Ireland. Student study centres are provided in nine locations.

Colleges of further education provide vocational courses for full-time, part-time and sandwich course students. In addition they organise basic education courses for adults who wish to have a second chance to learn. There are also non-vocational courses, mostly for adults, provided as part of leisure and which do not lead to any recognised qualification.

Two colleges of education—Stranmillis and St Mary's—are concerned solely with teacher education, mainly for primary schools. The training of teachers in secondary schools is largely provided by the education departments in the two universities.

There is a Youth Training Programme which is administered by the Training and Employment Agency, in partnership with the Department of Education (see p. 44).

Other Educational Services

The education and library boards also provide library services and secure the provision of recreational and youth service facilities. The district councils are responsible for providing facilities for recreational, social, physical and cultural activities.

The Department of Education provides financial support to a number of voluntary organisations working in the community relations field.

Health and Personal Social Services

Health and personal social services are fully integrated in Northern Ireland and correspond favourably with those available in the rest of Britain. They are administered by four health and social services boards on behalf of the Department of Health and Social Services. The Central Services Agency provides certain common services to the boards. Under the 1992–97 Regional

Strategy for Northern Ireland there are four main priorities, namely:

—a greater emphasis on health promotion and disease prevention;

—the continued improvement of acute hospital services;

—a shift from institutional care to care in the community; and

—targeting health and social need.

Health care is offered by doctors, dentists, opticians and pharmacists working within the Health Service as independent practitioners. Family doctors practise from modern and well-equipped health centres where medical and nursing services are provided. Some centres offer dental, pharmaceutical and eye care services.

Family doctors provide health checks for patients when they register with a doctor or if they have not seen their doctor for some time. They are encouraged to provide more health promotion clinics. Most doctors also provide free family planning services. Efforts are being made to combat cervical cancer and breast cancer by inviting all women between the ages of 20 and 64 for cervical screening by March 1993; all women in this age-group will be offered a test once every five years. A breast cancer screening programme is being introduced throughout Northern Ireland. All women aged between 50 and 64 will be invited for screening by March 1994 and will then be invited for screening every three years. Screening for women over 64 will be provided on request every three years.

Health services for young children include checks on height, weight and growth in the first five years of life.

For people over 75, family doctors offer an annual assessment of their health and circumstances.

Plans are being made to improve family doctor services through more convenient surgery hours, more comfortable waiting rooms, a wider range of professional staff such as nurses and physiotherapists, and the availability of minor surgery on doctors' own premises. Changing doctors is easier than it used to be and each practice produces leaflets about its services.

From April 1993 bigger family doctor practices will be able to choose to take control of funds to finance services for their own patients, including certain hospital treatments.

Free dental care is available for:

—children up to the age of 18 and students up to the age of 19;

—pregnant women and mothers of very young children; and

—people getting income support or family credit.

Health and social services boards are responsible for hospital care. The Government's charter for patients sets out the standards of care and treatment that they can expect when ill or in need of personal care and support. These include:

—a guarantee that virtually every patient who needs hospital treatment will be admitted to hospital within two years;

—guaranteed admission dates for patients whose operations have to be cancelled at the last minute because of emergencies or staff sickness;

—an end to block-bookings for hospital outpatient appointments, to ensure that each patient has an individual appointment time and is seen by the doctor within 30 minutes of the appointment;

—better discharge procedures so that patients are not discharged from hospital before arrangements have been made for their continuing care and treatment;

—assessments within seven days for people who need care and support in the community;

—better information about the services available and how to obtain them; and

—clear and effective arrangements for dealing with complaints.

The boards are to publish local charters providing more details about local services and standards. Details of current waiting times for admission to hospital will also be displayed in health centres and doctors' surgeries. The boards will have to publish each year information about their achievements against these standards and say what action they will be taking to improve performance where standards are not being met.

Under recent reforms hospitals and other units can choose to become a Health and Social Services Trust which will remain within the health and social services but be run by a Board of Directors. Trusts will be able to own their assets, employ their own staff, set their rates of pay and borrow money to develop their services. Before a Trust can be set up, all those with an interest will be asked for their views and have an opportunity to express an opinion. Trust services will continue to be free at the point of use since Trusts are not private hospitals.

Health and social services councils are being set up in each board area to represent the interests of the public and those who use the service. Forty per cent of membership is reserved for district councillors or district council nominees. The councils are involved in reviewing the operation of services in their area, making representations to boards for improving these and commenting on the boards' plans. The health and social services boards are required to consult Councils on proposals for any substantial development or change in the way services are provided.

State services are complemented by the voluntary organisations, many of which receive government grants. Examples include bodies providing playgroups for pre-school children or those assisting people to cope with a particular disability. Voluntary organisations may be staffed by professional and voluntary workers.

Social Security

The social security system is much the same as in the rest of Britain. The main types of benefit are:

—those paid in return for contributions, for example, retirement pension and benefits for sickness and unemployment, widowhood, maternity and industrial injuries;

—non-contributory benefits paid to certain groups such as disabled people, regardless of income;

—income support for people not in full-time work with incomes below specified levels; and

—family credit to help working people on low incomes with at least one child to support.

Housing benefit—rent rebates and allowances and rate rebates—are also available to people with low incomes, whether in work or not.

A social fund provides help to people, mainly those receiving income support, with exceptional expenses which may be difficult to meet from regular income; the help is mainly in the form of loans but there is provision for non-repayable community care grants and maternity and cold weather payments.

People on low incomes may be eligible for other financial assistance, for example, with health service charges and legal aid.

Housing

The Department of the Environment has overall responsibility for the formulation and direction of housing policy and works closely with the Northern Ireland Housing Executive on implementing public sector housing policy. The Executive is the only public housing authority in Northern Ireland and with its stock of some 163,000 homes accounts for almost a third of the total housing stock in the Province.

The Executive's main objectives are to:

—assess housing need and progressively to meet this by direct provision or by enabling other individuals or agencies to do so;

—promote high standards of new building, repair, maintenance, housing management and general housing advice; and

—strive to be the best public housing authority in Britain, measured in terms of quality and value for money.

When allocating homes, the Executive gives priority to those in greatest need. It has contracts with its customers in the form of tenancy agreements and published standards of service. In addition, all the Executive's tenants receive reports on the performance of their particular district offices. There are joint planning arrangements with health and social services boards to meet the needs of disabled people, for example, by providing specialist accommodation in new-build schemes, adapting existing homes or funding adaptations in the private sector.

The Executive has built 73,000 houses since its formation in 1971 and has completed improvements and repairs to 190,000 homes in the private sector.

Just over 64 per cent of homes in Northern Ireland are owner-occupied, compared with 54 per cent in 1981. The Executive's tenants have the right to buy their own home; its house sales policy has enabled over 50,000 tenants to purchase their home. A part-purchase, part-rental scheme, operated by the Northern Ireland Co-ownership Housing Association, has also enabled people to become home owners.

The Executive's work is complemented by the housing association movement, which is the main provider of purpose-built specialised housing for elderly and disabled people and for vulnerable and disadvantaged groups. This role will be developed further over the next few years. By the end of 1991 associations had completed 6,751 new homes and rehabilitated 2,866 existing ones.

The Media

Northern Ireland has two morning newspapers, one evening and three Sunday papers, all of which are published in Belfast. They are the *News Letter* (unionist), the *Irish News* (nationalist), the evening *Belfast Telegraph*, the *Sunday News*, *Sunday Life* and *Sunday World* (Northern Ireland edition). There are also about 45 weeklies.

Newspapers from the Irish Republic, as well as the British national press, are widely read in the province.

In addition to the national television and radio channels, there is a regional radio and television service run by the British Broadcasting Corporation (BBC) which also has a local radio station in Londonderry, Radio Foyle. An independent radio station, 'Downtown', is based in Newtownards, County Down, and broadcasts to the whole of Northern Ireland. There is also an independent programme company which provides a television service, financed by advertising and transmitting programmes from the national independent television network; special regional and news programmes are broadcast for people in Northern Ireland. Both BBC and independent television stations in the province produce programmes for national transmission throughout Britain. Satellite television is also available.

As part of its measures against terrorism, the Government has banned the broadcasting of direct statements made by people representing terrorist organisations.

Cultural and Social Life

Northern Ireland has a thriving cultural and social life which is appreciated by residents and visitors alike.

Leisure facilities, provided mainly by district councils with Government assistance, are among the best in Britain, with some 50 leisure centres and 40 indoor swimming pools. These are complemented by Northern Ireland's numerous natural amenities.

The Government supports the development of sport and physical recreation through the Sports Council for Northern Ireland which assists the many voluntary sports organisations.

Support for the arts is strong and there is a growing interest in the development of arts facilities in most of the main towns. Local arts festivals are a regular feature of the arts calendar, the highlight being the Belfast Festival based at Queen's University, which is one of the largest arts festivals in Britain. The restoration and reopening of the Grand Opera House in Belfast, at the start of the 1980s, made a major contribution to the social revival of Belfast city centre. Another success story has been the development of the Ulster Orchestra as a major musical force.

Government support for the arts is channelled through the Northern Ireland Arts Council which gives financial help and advice to opera and drama companies, orchestras and festivals, arts centres, touring theatres, writers and a wide variety of artistic groups and individuals. It also advises local authorities and education and library boards on arts projects and has its own gallery in Belfast.

The Association of Ulster Drama Festivals is the umbrella organisation for amateur drama festivals in the provinces. Opera is promoted by Opera Northern Ireland.

The province's heritage is preserved and portrayed by the Ulster Museum in Belfast and the Ulster Folk and Transport Museum at Holywood, County Down, and by a number of smaller local museums. The Ulster-American Folk Park in the west specialises in the history of Irish emigration to America, and is developing an extensive computer database on emigrants, which will be available for public access.

In 1989 a major grant programme was established relating to the cultural heritage of Northern Ireland. Its aim is to help people understand much more about what really happened in the past, about the history of their own locality and the different traditions which they have inherited. Such projects emphasise that there is much to share in Northern Ireland's cultural background, that diversity of traditions need not become a wedge separating communities and that sincerely held views need not be threatening or divisive.

Appendix: The 1985 Anglo-Irish Agreement and Selected Government Statements 1990–92

1: The 1985 Anglo-Irish Agreement

AGREEMENT BETWEEN THE GOVERNMENT OF THE UNITED KINGDOM OF GREAT BRITAIN AND NORTHERN IRELAND AND THE GOVERNMENT OF THE REPUBLIC OF IRELAND

The Government of the United Kingdom of Great Britain and Northern Ireland and the Government of the Republic of Ireland:

Wishing further to develop the unique relationship between their peoples and the close co-operation between their countries as friendly neighbours and as partners in the European Community;

Recognising the major interest of both their countries and, above all, of the people of Northern Ireland in diminishing the divisions there and achieving lasting peace and stability;

Recognising the need for continuing efforts to reconcile and to acknowledge the rights of the two major traditions that exist in Ireland, represented on the one hand by those who wish for no change in the present status of Northern Ireland and on the other hand by those who aspire to a sovereign united Ireland achieved by peaceful means and through agreement;

Reaffirming their total rejection of any attempt to promote political objectives by violence or the threat of violence and their determination to work together to ensure that those who adopt or support such methods do not succeed;

Recognising that a condition of genuine reconciliation and dialogue between unionists and nationalists is mutual recognition and acceptance of each other's rights;

Recognising and respecting the identities of the two communities in Northern Ireland, and the right of each to pursue its aspirations by peaceful and constitutional means;

Reaffirming their commitment to a society in Northern Ireland in which all may live in peace, free from discrimination and intolerance, and with the opportunity for both communities to participate fully in the structures and processes of government;

Have accordingly agreed as follows:

A: Status of Northern Ireland
ARTICLE 1

The two Governments

(a)   affirm that any change in the status of Northern Ireland would only come about with the consent of a majority of the people of Northern Ireland;

(b)   recognise that the present wish of a majority of the people of Northern Ireland is for no change in the status of Northern Ireland;

(c)   declare that, if in the future a majority of the people of Northern Ireland clearly wish for and formally consent to the establishment of a united Ireland, they will introduce and support in the respective Parliaments legislation to give effect to that wish.

B: The Intergovernmental Conference
ARTICLE 2

(a)   There is hereby established, within the framework of the Anglo-Irish Intergovernmental Council set up after the meeting between the two Heads of Government on 6 November 1981, an

Intergovernmental Conference (hereinafter referred to as 'the Conference'), concerned with Northern Ireland and with relations between the two parts of the island of Ireland, to deal, as set out in this Agreement, on a regular basis with

(i) political matters;

(ii) security and related matters;

(iii) legal matters, including the administration of justice;

(iv) the promotion of cross-border co-operation.

(b) The United Kingdom Government accepts that the Irish Government will put forward views and proposals on matters relating to Northern Ireland within the field of activity of the Conference in so far as those matters are not the responsibility of a devolved administration in Northern Ireland. In the interest of promoting peace and stability, determined efforts shall be made through the Conference to resolve any differences. The Conference will be mainly concerned with Northern Ireland; but some of the matters under consideration will involve co-operative action in both parts of the island of Ireland, and possibly also in Great Britain. Some of the proposals considered in respect of Northern Ireland may also be found to have application by the Irish Government. There is no derogation from the sovereignty of either the United Kingdom Government or the Irish Government, and each retains responsibility for the decisions and administration of government within its own jurisdiction.

Article 3

The Conference shall meet at Ministerial or official level, as required. The business of the Conference will thus receive attention at the highest level. Regular and frequent Ministerial meetings shall be held; and in particular special meetings shall be convened at the request of either side. Officials may meet in subordinate groups. Membership of the Conference and of sub-groups shall be small and flexible. When the Conference meets at Ministerial level the Secretary of State for Northern Ireland and an Irish Minister designated as the

Permanent Irish Ministerial Representative shall be joint Chairmen. Within the framework of the Conference other British and Irish Ministers may hold or attend meetings as appropriate: when legal matters are under consideration the Attorneys General may attend. Ministers may be accompanied by their officials and their professional advisers: for example, when questions of security policy or security co-operation are being discussed, they may be accompanied by the Chief Constable of the Royal Ulster Constabulary and the Commissioner of the Garda Siochana; or when questions of economic or social policy or co-operation are being discussed, they may be accompanied by officials of the relevant Departments. A Secretariat shall be established by the two Governments to service the Conference on a continuing basis in the discharge of its functions as set out in this Agreement.

ARTICLE 4

(a)   In relation to matters coming within its field of activity, the Conference shall be a framework within which the United Kingdom Government and the Irish Government work together

(i)   for the accommodation of the rights and identities of the two traditions which exist in Northern Ireland; and

(ii)   for peace, stability and prosperity throughout the island of Ireland by promoting reconciliation, respect for human rights, co-operation against terrorism and the development of economic, social and cultural co-operation.

(b)   It is the declared policy of the United Kingdom Government that responsibility in respect of certain matters within the powers of the Secretary of State for Northern Ireland should be devolved within Northern Ireland on a basis which would secure widespread acceptance throughout the community. The Irish Government support that policy.

(c)   Both Governments recognise that devolution can be achieved only with the co-operation of constitutional representatives within Northern Ireland of both traditions there. The Conference shall be a framework within which the Irish Government may put forward views and proposals on the modalities of bringing about devolution in Northern Ireland, in so far as they relate to the interests of the minority community.

C: Political Matters

ARTICLE 5

(a)   The Conference shall concern itself with measures to recognise and accommodate the rights and identities of the two traditions in Northern Ireland, to protect human rights and to prevent discrimination. Matters to be considered in this area include measures to foster the cultural heritage of both traditions, changes in electoral arrangements, the use of flags and emblems, the avoidance of economic and social discrimination and the advantages and disadvantages of a Bill of Rights in some form in Northern Ireland.

(b)   The discussion of these matters shall be mainly concerned with Northern Ireland, but the possible application of any measures pursuant to this Article by the Irish Government in their jurisdiction shall not be excluded.

(c)   If it should prove impossible to achieve and sustain devolution on a basis which secures widespread acceptance in Northern Ireland, the Conference shall be a framework within which the Irish Government may, where the interests of the minority community are significantly or especially affected, put forward views on proposals for major legislation and on major policy issues, which are within the purview of the Northern Ireland Departments and which remain the responsibility of the Secretary of State for Northern Ireland.

ARTICLE 6

The Conference shall be a framework within which the Irish Government may put forward views and proposals on the role and composition of bodies appointed by the Secretary of State for Northern

Ireland or by Departments subject to his direction and control including

the Standing Advisory Commission on Human Rights;

the Fair Employment Agency;

the Equal Opportunities Commission;

the Police Authority for Northern Ireland;

the Police Complaints Board.

D: Security and Related Matters

ARTICLE 7

(a) The Conference shall consider

(i) security policy;

(ii) relations between the security forces and the community;

(iii) prisons policy.

(b) The Conference shall consider the security situation at its regular meetings and thus provide an opportunity to address policy issues, serious incidents and forthcoming events.

(c) The two Governments agree that there is a need for a programme of special measures in Northern Ireland to improve relations between the security forces and the community, with the object in particular of making the security forces more readily accepted by the nationalist community. Such a programme shall be developed, for the Conference's consideration, and may include the establishment of local consultative machinery, training in community relations, crime prevention schemes involving the community, improvements in arrangements for handling complaints, and action to increase the proportion of members of the minority in the Royal Ulster Constabulary. Elements of the programme may be considered by the Irish Government suitable for application within their jurisdiction.

(d) The Conference may consider policy issues relating to prisons. Individual cases may be raised as appropriate, so that information can be provided or inquiries instituted.

E: Legal Matters, Including the Administration of Justice

ARTICLE 8

The Conference shall deal with issues of concern to both countries relating to the enforcement of the criminal law. In particular it shall consider whether there are areas of the criminal law applying in the North and in the South respectively which might with benefit be harmonised. The two Governments agree on the importance of public confidence in the administration of justice. The Conference shall seek, with the help of advice from experts as appropriate, measures which would give substantial expression to this aim, considering *inter alia* the possibility of mixed courts in both jurisdictions for the trial of certain offences. The Conference shall also be concerned with policy aspects of extradition and extra-territorial jurisdiction as between North and South.

F: Cross-Border Co-operation on Security, Economic, Social and Cultural Matters

ARTICLE 9

(a)   With a view to enhancing cross-border co-operation on security matters, the Conference shall set in hand a programme of work to be undertaken by the Chief Constable of the Royal Ulster Constabulary and the Commissioner of the Garda Siochana and, where appropriate, groups of officials, in such areas as threat assessments, exchange of information, liaison structures, technical co-operation, training of personnel, and operational resources.

(b)   The Conference shall have no operational responsibilities; responsibility for police operations shall remain with the heads of the respective police forces, the Chief Constable of the Royal Ulster Constabulary maintaining his links with the Secretary of State for Northern Ireland and the Commissioner of the Garda Siochana his links with the Minister for Justice.

ARTICLE 10

(a)   The two Governments shall co-operate to promote the economic and social development of those areas of both parts of Ireland which have suffered most severely from the consequences of the instability of recent years, and shall consider the possibility of securing international support for this work.

(b) If it should prove impossible to achieve and sustain devolution on a basis which secures widespread acceptance in Northern Ireland, the Conference shall be a framework for the promotion of co-operation between the two parts of Ireland concerning cross-border aspects of economic, social and cultural matters in relation to which the Secretary of State for Northern Ireland continues to exercise authority.

(c) If responsibility is devolved in respect of certain matters in the economic, social or cultural areas currently within the responsibility of the Secretary of State for Northern Ireland, machinery will need to be established by the responsible authorities in the North and South for practical co-operation in respect of cross-border aspects of these issues.

G: Arrangements for Review

ARTICLE 11

At the end of three years from signature of this Agreement, or earlier if requested by either Government, the working of the Conference shall be reviewed by the two Governments to see whether any changes in the scope and nature of its activities are desirable.

H: Interparliamentary Relations

ARTICLE 12

It will be for Parliamentary decision in Westminster and in Dublin whether to establish an Anglo-Irish Parliamentary body of the kind adumbrated in the Anglo-Irish Studies Report of November 1981. The two Governments agree that they would give support as appropriate to such a body, if it were to be established.

I: Final Clauses

ARTICLE 13

This Agreement shall enter into force on the date on which the two Governments exchange notifications of their acceptance of this Agreement.

In witness whereof the undersigned, being duly authorised thereto by their respective Governments, have signed this Agreement.

Done in two originals at Hillsborough on the 15th day of November 1985

For the Government of
the United Kingdom
of Great Britain and
Northern Ireland

For the Government of
the Republic of Ireland

2: Speech made by the Northern Ireland Secretary, Mr Peter Brooke, on 9 January 1990

I said before Christmas that I sensed that there was a new mood developing in the electorate of Northern Ireland and their politicians. I believed that it was just possible that the will might exist to achieve some political progress in the near future. I want today to reflect further on how that progress might now be made.

For some months now I have been talking and listening—as Brian Mawhinney has also been doing, and as we shall continue to do—to politicians in Northern Ireland and others who are influential in their communities. I should like to share with you some of the impressions we have formed.

There is no doubt, it seems to me, that support for constitutional politics remains strong in Northern Ireland. That is so despite the terrorist campaign and the lack of major progress so far towards a political accommodation between the two traditions. Yet some progress has been made, I do believe, by a variety of initiatives and by the good will of many individuals, towards healing the divisions within the community. We all welcome that and want to see further progress. And many politicians in Northern Ireland see the need for both sides of the community to work together at the political level. They see the direct benefits that would arise for the community as a whole from local accountability for government functions.

While I and my colleagues will continue to do all that we can to deliver good government to the people of Northern Ireland, there is a limit to what we can achieve without the greater involvement of locally elected representatives.

Perhaps the most striking feature of the local political scene is the absence of a forum here in which local politicians can help to find solutions to the problems which face those they represent. I feel that absence keenly. But I suggest that the absence of such a forum is, or should be, most keenly felt by local politicians themselves and those whom they represent. Certainly, the discussions which I have held with politicians do suggest that there continues to be widespread support for the devolution of legislative and executive powers, although some favour more limited initial steps in that direction.

I should like to say a little more about how I see the current position.

I have been listening carefully to what Unionist politicians have been saying. I am sure that, like all democratic politicians, they want to be involved in action and not just in words. I understand of course their overriding concern which is, by definition, to see the Union preserved, and I hope that I understand, if I do not share, the feelings they have expressed about the Anglo-Irish Agreement. I do not believe they would serve their own interests, or those of the people they represent, by some sort of internal exile. And I have noted the increasing emphasis of Unionists in what they have been saying on the need for them to share more fully in decision-taking, whether at Westminster or more locally.

Although there are differing views about the form and extent of devolution, there does seem to be a common recognition that there is a real need for powers to be devolved, and that any form of devolution must involve a proper role for both sides of the Northern Ireland community. Unionists have also made clear that they accept that there needs to be a good and neighbourly relationship between any new Northern Ireland administration and the Republic of Ireland, and a similarly good relationship between the United Kingdom and the Republic.

The leadership of the two main Unionist parties have told me that they stand by the 'outline proposal' which they put to Mr King almost two years ago for a replacement of the Anglo-Irish Agreement. Their ideas about the future government of Northern Ireland were subsequently described by the Prime Minister as a 'constructive' and 'encouraging' starting-point for talks between the Northern Ireland political parties.

I therefore welcome the continuing commitment of the Unionist leadership to seek progress from that starting-point. I also welcome the concern of other Unionist politicians to develop their thinking on these lines and to find ways to enable talks between the parties to start. I recognise that Unionists have been seeking a commitment from the Government to consider a replacement to the Agreement, and that they would like the workings of the Agreement to be suspended for a temporary period to enable political talks to start.

However, my main impression from contacts with Unionist politicians is the strength of interest which exists in seeking a better form of government for Northern Ireland, in which local elected representatives—from both sides of the community—can share on a basis which is fair to all. Detailed proposals for a new devolved administration have been put forward in the past, and take various forms, some of them reflected in the constitutional legislation which remains on the statute books. The most recent proposals to be published are in fact those of the Alliance Party, which has for many years argued forcefully for devolution on a basis which gives an appropriate share in power to both communities.

The SDLP for its part fully supports the Anglo-Irish Agreement and the relationship of trust and co-operation between the two governments which it represents, particularly because of the reassurance which the Agreement provides to the nationalist community. In recent months SDLP politicians have themselves been stressing the advantages of a devolved form of government in which both sides of the community would be represented. They acknowledge the importance of bridging the communal divide and creating a system of government in which representatives of the two communities can work successfully together. The SDLP accepts that Unionists wish to retain their own political and cultural identity, as nationalists do theirs. They recognise, and have said forcefully, that progress can only be achieved through a dialogue. SDLP politicians have stressed to me that they are keen to help to bring that about and to participate in it fully, with a view to achieving devolution. I welcome this and look forward to a more detailed and developed expression of their views.

It does appear, however, that common ground exists about the major issues which talks between the political parties would need to address. There need to be devised workable and acceptable arrangements for the exercise of developed powers over a range of matters. There needs to be agreement on democratic institutions which would give appropriate weight to majority and minority aspirations and views. There is the question which is addressed by the Anglo-Irish Agreement: how the legitimate interest of the Irish Government in matters within Northern Ireland, particularly as regards the minority community, are to be acknowledged, without dilution of UK sovereignty or the status of Northern Ireland as part of the United Kingdom. And there is the question of a local political contribution to security matters.

It is of course for the parties themselves in the first instance to say wheher these issues might usefully form the bones of an agenda for talks between them. I shall be very willing to give them any help that they want in setting that agenda, but I do suggest that there are certain realities which they cannot ignore. And the prospects for eventual agreement will depend on the politicians themselves. Some of their aspirations may be different, but it may be that the practical differences which divide them are not unbridgeable. Perhaps I could set out some of the principles which might guide them and the government in seeking a way forward.

Northern Ireland will not cease to be a part of the United Kingdom without the consent of a majority of the people who live here. That has been the position in British law for 40 years and it is reinforced by Article 1 of the Anglo-Irish Agreement. Majority desire for a change in status clearly does not exist at present and seems unlikely in the foreseeable future. That is the reality which I believe that all constitutional politicians in Northern Ireland in practice accept.

Within that constitutional framework, therefore, the Government will continue to seek, for all the people of Northern Ireland, the fruits of peace, order and good government. All the constitutional political parties also share those objectives, and they are likely to be best served by the greater localisation of political power.

We therefore seek institutions of government in Northern Ireland which will be directly accountable to the people of Northern Ireland—to all its people—and to which they can give their wholehearted commitment and support. The Government has not prejudged the detailed form that any such political arrangements should take. Those arrangements which local politicians are expected to work they must help create. Our only broad criteria for endorsing any particular arrangement which might be proposed are that it should be workable, and likely to prove stable and durable, and that it must command widespread support and provide an appropriate and fair role for both sides of the community.

It seems likely in practice that the best hope of this lies through a devolved Province-wide administration and legislature, though the Government will look seriously at any proposal that is workable and could achieve widespread support. The policy of devolution is not of course a new one. It pre-dates the Agreement. Indeed, it has been the policy of successive British governments since 1972. The powers to be devolved can only be decided, after appropriate consultation, by the British Government and Parliament. It is simply not true, as some assert, that Article 4 of the Agreement gives the Irish Government some sort of veto. The authority rests with Parliament at Westminster.

Matters transferred to a new developed administration would of course be outside the purview of the Intergovernmental Conference. To those who doubt that the Agreement permits this, I should point out that, on the contrary, the Agreement provides for it. The relationship between any new Northern Ireland administration and the Irish authorities would of course be an issue for discussions involving both parties.

Finally, I would say this about our general approach. There can be no denying the existence of the two main traditions in Northern Ireland and the need for each to respect the other and to be given its proper place. The Anglo-Irish Agreement represents an honest attempt to grapple with that reality, without confusing the constitutional reality of continued UK sovereignty, and, since the nationalist community regards itself at least in part as Irish, it is natural and can be helpful that there should be an Irish dimension to Northern Irish affairs. Let us remember too, and I say this not only to Unionists, that the different traditions can be a source of strength and vitality, rather than division and weakness.

Against that background, how can we now make progress? I have sought to indicate the issues which need to be discussed between the parties and the principles which might inform our and their approach. The problems we face together can only be resolved by the political parties talking together and with the Government.

The Government has said—and I repeat—that we set no preconditions for such talks. I have recognised that some may join the discussions, intending to raise issues for consideration which we would not necessarily wish to raise ourselves, and I have also made it clear that I am always ready to consider constructive proposals particularly where they enjoy a wide measure of support. It seems self-evident that discussions about the future government of Northern Ireland would need to embrace both the concept of devolution and the North–South relationship, and it is impossible to ignore the wider relationship between the two islands.

There can be no doubt that in practice, any agreement between the constitutional political parties on new arrangements for exercising political power in Northern Ireland would have substantial implications for the Anglo-Irish Agreement, and both Governments would,

I believe, be bound to consider those implications seriously and sympathetically. The two Governments have already stated formally that, if in future it appeared that the objectives of the Agreement could more effectively be served by changes in the scope and nature of the working of the Conference, the two Governments would be willing in principle to consider making such changes. I do believe, as we have often said, that the agreement can be operated sensitively, in the interests of bringing about talks between the political parties and giving them the best possible chance of success.

But so much depends on the will of politicians and those they represent to seek agreement between them. There is already a substantial exchange of views between local politicians and the Government about how progress might now be made. I hope that very soon all the main constitutional political parties will be involved in such exchanges with the Government, and with each other, on these very important matters. I stand ready to facilitate agreement on the arrangements for inter-party talks, and to discuss the steps the Government might take to help.

I would not wish to raise hopes unduly. Much work needs to be done, but there may now in my judgement be enough common ground to make worthwhile the start of talks soon on new arrangements for exercising political power within Northern Ireland. I do hope that politicians here will make the most of the opportunity which may now exist. I look forward to their considered responses to what I have had to say.

Public commitments to political progress—and private ones— are no substitute for engaging in genuine political dialogue. The eventual prize for success in such a dialogue would be a form of government which was widely acceptable and contributed substantially to long term political stability. Local politicians, by demonstrating *their ability to work together, would be helping to bring an end to terrorism. A successful devolved government would of course also improve Northern Ireland's image as a location for investment and business expansion, and help us to attract the new jobs that we want to see for all in the community. It would help all the people of Northern Ireland to tackle and reduce the divisions between the two sides of the community. And it would in particular ensure that decisions about the day-to-day business of government would be more directly responsive to local needs and requirements.*

3: House of Commons Statement, 26 March 1991, by Mr Brooke regarding the opening of political talks

Mr Speaker, I am pleased to be able to inform the House that, following extensive discussions with the main constitutional political parties in Northern Ireland—the Alliance Party of Northern Ireland, the Social Democratic and Labour Party, the Ulster Democratic Unionist Party and the Ulster Unionist Party—and with the Irish Government, a basis for formal political talks now exists. I frankly acknowledge to the House that this would not have been possible without the goodwill and determination of the Northern Ireland parties and the helpful and constructive approach taken by the Irish Government. The stated positions of all these parties are well known. Her Majesty's Government reaffirms its position that North-ern Ireland's present status as a part of the United Kingdom will not change without the consent of a majority of its people.

The endeavour on which we have all agreed to embark is an ambitious one. We are setting out to achieve a new beginning for relationships within Northern Ireland, within the island of Ireland and between the peoples of these islands. While a successful outcome cannot be guaranteed in advance, I am confident that all the potential participants are committed to a forward-looking and constructive approach. For their part, the two signatories of the Anglo-Irish Agreement—the British and Irish Governments—have made clear that they would be prepared to consider a new and more broadly based agreement or structure if such an arrangement can be arrived at through direct discussion and negotiation between all of the parties concerned.

To allow an opportunity for such a wider political dialogue the two Governments have agreed not to hold a meeting of the Anglo-Irish Conference between two pre-specified dates. All of the parties concerned will make use of this interval for intensive discussions to seek the new and more broadly based agreement which I have just described.

As the Conference will not be meeting between the specified dates the Secretariat at Maryfield will accordingly not be required for that period to discharge its normal role of servicing Conference meetings provided for in Article 3 of the Agreement.

It is accepted that discussions must focus on three main relationships: those within Northern Ireland, including the relation-ship between any new institutions there and the Westminster Parlia-ment; among the people of the island of Ireland; and between the two Governments. It is common ground between all the parties that hope of achieving a new and more broadly based agreement rests on finding a way to give adequate expression to the totality of the relationships I have mentioned.

Talks will accordingly take place in three strands corresponding respectively to the three relationships. Some arrangement will be needed for liaison between the different strands of these complex discussions. All the Northern Ireland parties will participate actively and directly in the North–South discussions. The Unionist parties have made clear that they wish their participation in those talks to be formally associated with my presence and that they will regard themselves as members of the United Kingdom team.

It is accepted by all those involved that, so as to make full use of the interval between meetings of the Conference to achieve an overall agreement satisfactory to all, it will be necessary to have launched all three sets of discussions within weeks of each other.

A first step towards getting related discussions under way in all three strands will be the opening, as soon as possible, of substantive talks between the parties in Northern Ireland under my chairmanship. These will commence with a round of bilateral meetings before moving on, as soon as possible, into plenary sessions. It has been agreed by all the participants that before long, when, after consultation, I judge that an appropriate point has been reached, I will propose formally that the other two strands should be launched. My judgement as to timing will be governed by the fact that all involved have agreed that the three sets of discussions will be under way within weeks of each other.

The internal talks, like the talks in the other strands, will follow a demanding and intensive schedule. In order to ensure a full airing of the issues, it will be open to each of the parties to raise any aspect of these relationships including constitutional issues, or any other matter which it considers relevant. All concerned have assured me that they will participate in good faith and will make every effort to achieve progress.

It is accepted by all the parties that nothing will be finally agreed in any strand until everything is agreed in the talks as a whole and that confidentiality will be maintained thereunto. However, in the final analysis the outcome will need to be acceptable to the people.

4: House of Commons Statement, 3 July 1991, by Mr Brooke on the conclusion of political talks

The political talks which have been taking place at Parliament buildings, Stormont, have been brought to a conclusion. I should like to take this opportunity to explain to the House the background to that decision, to describe what has been achieved during the talks and to set out the Government's hopes for the future.

Hon. Members will recall that my statement to the House on 26 March was accepted as a basis for political talks which would address, as part of the same process, relationships within Northern Ireland, including the relationship between any new institutions there and the Westminster Parliament; relationships among the people of the island of Ireland; and relationships between the two Governments. I announced that talks would take place in three strands corresponding to those three main sets of relationships. To allow an opportunity for the wider political dialogue which the four main constitutional political parties in Northern Ireland and the two Governments envisaged, the two Governments had agreed not to hold a meeting of the Anglo-Irish Conference between two pre-specified dates, subsequently confirmed as being 26 April and 16 July. This interval, allowing some time at each end for the Anglo-Irish secretariat to complete the business of servicing one conference meeting and to make preparations to service the next, provided 10 clear weeks for substantive political exchanges. The talks began on 30 April.

It became clear that it would not be possible to launch the other strands of the talks and thus to complete the process as a whole before the end of that interval, and that that was beginning to inhibit our ability to make further substantive progress. After consultation with the leaders of the political parties, I concluded that the talks should therefore be brought to an end. I have also been in touch with the Irish Government to recount my conclusion.

I should now like to take stock of what has been achieved during the talks and of the further prospects for securing constructive political development in relation to Northern Ireland. As the House knows, it did not prove possible to move as rapidly as we had hoped to plenary sessions of the first strand of the talks. A range of new procedural issues had to be resolved. A series of bilateral exchanges succeeded in determining the venues for meetings in the second strand of the talks, arrangements for chairing that strand of discussion, the identity of the chairman and the procedural guidelines which would be observed.

Plenary sessions started on 17 June. After my opening statement, the parties presented their initial position papers, after which the papers were discussed, examined and clarified. Subsequently, during a more intensive schedule of meetings, there was a debate on themes that had emerged from the initial presentations.

The commitment and seriousness of purpose shown by all the parties in these talks is a source of encouragement for the future. The plenary sessions provided the forum for some significant and constructive exchanges among the parties and with Her Majesty's Government on a range of fundamental issues. The nature of those exchanges served to confirm the judgment involved in initiating the talks process that the time is ripe for political talks in relation to Northern Ireland that address all the relevant relationships; that the process is of value and has potentially even greater value; that a degree of common ground exists; and that there is a good prospect that a comprehensive political accommodation can be reached. I would like to express my appreciation of the commitment shown by all the participants.

To those who would say, 'I told you so—it would never work,' I offer the reality of the past few weeks. While I am naturally disappointed at this moment that the current process has to end, foundations have been laid for progress in the future which neither cynics nor the men of violence will be able to undermine.

For myself, I hope that it will prove possible in due course to have further exchanges with the parties, and with the Irish Government, to explore, initially on a bilateral basis, whether we can establish terms on which fresh discussions could be held.

5: Agreed statement on political talks made by the parties on 27 January 1992

The Secretary of State for Northern Ireland, the Rt Hon Peter Brooke MP, accompanied by the Minister of State, Dr Brian Mawhinney MP, today met the leaders of the four main constitutional political parties in Northern Ireland, the Rt Hon James Molyneaux MP, Mr John Hume MP MEP, Dr Ian Paisley MP MEP, and Dr John Alderdice.

Together they reviewed the outcome of the round of discussions which have taken place since last September in the search for agreement on a basis for fresh political talks. They reasserted their support for a process of talks based on the statement of 26 March. However, they concluded with regret that it was not possible in present circumstances to proceed to launch fresh substantive talks on the lines envisaged.

They agreed that the various exchanges which had taken place over the past two years had been valuable in producing a basis for political dialogue which retained great potential and had yet to be fully exploited. They recalled the talks which took place between the parties in June and July last year and reaffirmed the view that these had produced genuine dialogue and provided a firm foundation for further substantive exchanges in due course. They expressed the hope that this would be taken further at the appropriate time.

The party leaders agreed that, in the meantime, at the invitation of the Secretary of State, they would meet to consider matters of common concern, including in the economic field, in the interests of all the people of Northern Ireland. They also agreed to respond to an invitation to field party teams to take part, for information, in intensive factual briefings, under the chairmanship of the Minister of State, on present financial and other administrative arrangements affecting the people of Northern Ireland.

The party leaders expressed the hope that by continuing to work together and by making representations together on matters of common concern they would contribute to the growth of mutual trust and confidence within the community in Northern Ireland, which would eventually aid the talks process.

6: House of Commons speech, 5 March 1992, by Mr Brooke

I am very glad that we are having this debate today. It is taking place at the request of the leaders of three of the main constitutional parties in Northern Ireland and is of a somewhat different nature from our usual debates. Normally, they take place in connection with a particular piece of legislation or in response to events in the Province. On this occasion, we have a welcome opportunity for a wide-ranging, and, perhaps, more reflective debate. I propose to keep my remarks relatively brief, but it may assist the House, if I give a general appraisal of the Government's general approach.

It is a paradox that, despite the vicious terrorist attacks which occur in Northern Ireland, there have been numerous studies over the years that have shown the Province to be among the most socially stable and law-abiding communities in the western democracies. There are strong local communities and a long tradition of good neighbourli-ness. Northern Ireland people are known for their work ethic and their strong Christian values. Northern Ireland has achievements in the industrial, agricultural, academic, medical and other spheres of which it can justifiably be proud . . .

Northern Ireland has the lowest rate of infant mortality in the United Kingdom and one of the highest rates of success in renal transplants. We lead the world in certain neuro-surgical techniques. In mathematics, Northern Ireland children at 11 and 15 outperform their counterparts in England and Wales. They get better results more generally at A-level and contribute to the highest level of participation in higher education in the United Kingdom where, again, success at national level attends them. The uptake of the Duke of Edinburgh award scheme is higher in Northern Ireland than in England and Wales, as is charity giving. Levels of indoor sport participation are the highest in the United Kingdom. Northern Ireland pioneered the vertical take-off jet, the modern farm tractor, the ejection seat, the portable heart defibrillator, the 4-wheel drive and the pneumatic tyre. I am told that tonic water was also invented there, to the benefit of sobriety throughout the world.

At the same time, overlying those attributes are the stresses of which we are all aware. Those arise from the fact that Northern Ireland is a divided society. Perhaps the most fundamental, structural problem in Northern Ireland is how to create the conditions where all sections of the community can live together in harmony. If that fundamental issue can be addressed successfully, it would lay a firm foundation for lasting peace in the Province. Much has been achieved in recent years to reduce historical suspicions and to address the sources of tension between the two main parts of the community. All of us who are familiar with Northern Ireland know that in many of their daily activities people from different parts of the community live, work and play happily side by side. I agree with those who say that, in Northern Ireland, diversity can and should be a source of strength and not weakness.

In this context, I should like to pay a warm and unreserved tribute to the people of Northern Ireland from this Dispatch Box. They have, for the past 20 years, had to withstand the most vicious terrorist compaigns waged by extremists on both sides of the community. Throughout that time, they have remained firm and resolute in their determination that those who use violence shall not have their way; their courage is a signal to us all. It is, moreover, a direct message to the terrorists themselves: the community has rejected and stood firm against them. After more than 20 years, the terrorists are absolutely no nearer to achieving their objectives . . .

I referred in my earlier remarks to the fact that Northern Ireland is a divided society. I said that the most fundamental structural issue facing any Government was how to close the community divisions. Those divisions have, to an extent, been reflected in economic and social disparities. Members from both sides of the community have felt that their political interests have been overridden in the past. The nature of the divisions raises the issues of constitutional status and personal and national identity . . .

At the heart of all those issues lies the need to tackle Northern Ireland's political problems. The requirement is to address the constitutional, economic and social grievances which perpetuate division and allow room for terrorism. At present, locally accountable and democratic institutions of government are almost entirely absent. As the House will know, the Government's objective is to seek to transfer greater political power and responsibility to locally elected representatives in Northern Ireland on a widely acceptable basis. If there is to be genuine reconciliation, different shades of constitutional political opinion must be accommodated in the political process . . .

The Government have also taken the view that no political accommodation in relation to Northern Ireland could be stable and durable if it addressed only internal arrangements for the government of Northern Ireland. That is why, with the support of our partners in dialogue, including the Irish Government, we have sought to construct a basis for political talks which could address, as part of the same process, relationships within Northern Ireland, including the relationship between any new institutions there and the Westminster Parliament; relationships among the people of the island of Ireland; and relationships between the two Governments.

Any such process was always bound to be difficult to establish. However, it has the enormous advantage that it can address all the relevant dimensions of the political problems of Northern Ireland, and I believe the various advantages of that have been widely recognised . . .

In short, as the party leaders acknowledged when I met them on 27 January, the talks process launched last March has considerable potential. It provides a realistic route towards a comprehensive political accommodation which could be of benefit to everyone, except the gunmen. All the constitutional political parties involved have something to gain from the talks process and the people of Northern Ireland have the most to gain . . .

When the talks ended last July, I said that, in my view, they had laid a firm foundation for the future. Since then, I have had further discussions with the party leaders and the Irish Government to see whether we could agree a return to the negotiating table. When it appeared, a few weeks ago, that that was unlikely, my Right Hon. Friend the Prime Minister invited the party leaders to discuss the issues with him. As a result of that meeting, they agreed to see whether a way round the obstacles could be found.

I am sure that the whole House will have been heartened by their statement last Friday that, subject to receiving written confirmation of the positions of the Prime Minister and the Leader of the Opposition, they could see no obstacle to the resumption of talks as soon as possible. I understand that the necessary assurances have now been given. I shall be discussing this with the Irish Foreign Minister, Mr Andrews, tomorrow, in the expectation that substantive talks will begin very soon.

It is not always recognised that elected representatives of the two parts of the community in Northern Ireland work together and amicably, both in this House and in the European Parliament, on a wide range of issues affecting all the people of the Province. My Right Hon. Friends the Prime Minister and the Secretary of State for Defence and I have recently benefited from a discussion of security issues with the four party leaders and I have this week had a further, productive meeting with them to discuss employment creation.

I believe that the formula that we have agreed between us provides a sound basis for tackling the issues. It ensures that all the relevant relationships are taken into account; that any party can raise any matter which it considers relevant, including constitutional issues; that nothing can be agreed in any one strand until there is agreement on all three strands as a whole; that there can be no change in the constitutional status of Northern Ireland as a part of the United Kingdom without the consent of a majority of its people; and that a new and more broadly based agreement or structure could emerge from the negotiations.

The past few years have seen the development of a close relationship between the United Kingdom and the Republic of Ireland. That has centred around our joint experience of operating the Anglo-Irish Agreement, to which the Government remain fully committed. The relationship has brought benefits to both countries in terms of economic and social development, co-operation in the fight against terrorism, and commitment to political progress in Northern Ireland. I am confident that the constructive relationship can be further strengthened in the months ahead.

I shall not seek to predict the nature of any new agreement that might evolve from future talks, but I believe that the pursuit of that agreement will be substantially assisted by our close relationship with the Republic of Ireland. I commend the Irish Government's constructive interest in the talks process and regard as helpful the Taoiseach's recent confirmation that, so far as their own involvement in new talks is concerned, everything will be on the table for discussion, including articles 2 and 3 of the Irish constitution.

Security co-operation is a vital component in the Anglo-Irish relationship. The threat posed by terrorism is never predictable and we must continuously review and refine cross-border co-operation to keep on top of that threat. But terrorism must never be allowed to dictate the agenda. There is important work to be done in developing the social and economic structure of Northern Ireland. Here, too, close relations with the Republic of Ireland are valuable. That is not something Governments can achieve alone. It is also for individual companies and private organisations to recognise the benefits that can be brought about by closer co-operation and to take the necessary steps to bring that about.

7: Agreed statement on political talks made by the parties on 9 March 1992

The first plenary meetings of the first strand of the new political talks took place at Parliament Buildings, Stormont, on Monday 9th March. The Secretary of State for Northern Ireland, the Rt Hon Peter Brooke MP, chaired the meetings, supported by the Minister of State, Dr Brian Mawhinney MP. The Rt Hon James Molyneaux MP, Mr John Hume

MP MEP, the Reverend Dr Ian Paisley MP MEP and Dr John Alderdice led delegations from the Ulster Unionist Party, the Social Democratic and Labour Party, the Ulster Democratic Unionist Party and the Alliance Party respectively.

The Secretary of State reported the Prime Minister's good wishes, conveyed this morning, which the participants noted with appreciation.

All the participants warmly welcomed the start of the new talks and looked forward to frank and constructive exchanges in the months ahead. They emphasised their determination to work together within the framework set out in the Secretary of State's statement to the House of Commons on 26 March 1991.

The parties confirmed that the talks would continue up to the point when the UK general election was called and that they would then resume after a post-election meeting of the Anglo-Irish Intergovernmental Conference.

The participants agreed on the need for arrangements to ensure swift and effective progress. To this end, a Business Committee was established to plan for the efficient conduct of business at future meetings. The Committee will comprise representatives of each delegation and be chaired by the Minister. It was agreed that the committee would meet immediately in preparation for the next plenary meeting.

8: Extract from Joint Statement of the Anglo-Irish Intergovernmental Conference, 27 April 1992

The Conference reviewed political developments since its last meeting on 6 March 1992 and confirmed that, to allow a further opportunity for talks to take place on the basis announced by the former Secretary of State in the House of Commons on 26 March 1991, there will be no further meeting of the Conference before the week beginning 27 July 1992. Both sides reaffirmed their commitment to the principles and terms of the 26 March 1991 statement. The two Governments expressed the strong hope that, with the co-operation of all involved, this further opportunity for talks will achieve a new beginning for relationships with Northern Ireland, within the island of Ireland and between the peoples of these islands.

Addresses

Northern Ireland Information Service, Stormont Castle, Belfast BT4 3ST.

Department of Agriculture, Dundonald House, Upper Newtownards Road, Belfast BT4 3SB.

Department of Economic Development, Netherleigh, Massey Avenue, Belfast BT4 2JP.

Department of Education, Rathgael House, Balloo Road, Bangor, County Down BT12 2PR.

Department of the Environment, Parliament Buildings, Stormont, Belfast BT4 3SS.

Department of Finance and Personnel, Parliament Buildings, Stormont, Belfast BT4 3SW.

Department of Health and Social Services, Dundonald House, Upper Newtownards Road, Belfast BT4 3SF.

Fair Employment Commission, Andras House, 60 Great Victoria Street, Belfast BT2 7BB.

Industrial Development Board, 64 Chichester Street, Belfast BT1 4JX.

International Fund for Ireland, PO Box 2000, Belfast.

Local Enterprise Development Unit, LEDU House, Upper Galwally, Belfast BT8 4TB.

Training and Employment Agency, Clarendon House, Adelaide Street, Belfast BT2 8DJ.

Printed in the United Kingdom for HMSO.
Dd 0294190 7/91 C30 51-2423 20249